Reading Walter de la Mare

Reading
Walter de la Mare

Poems Selected and Annotated
by William Wootten

faber

First published in 2021
by Faber & Faber Ltd
Bloomsbury House
74–77 Great Russell Street
London WC1B 3DA

Typeset by Typo•glyphix, Burton-on-Trent DE14 3HE
Printed in the UK by TJ Books Ltd, Padstow, Cornwall

A CIP record for this book
is available from the British Library

ISBN 978–0–571–34713–1

2 4 6 8 10 9 7 5 3 1

Contents

Acknowledgements

I should like to thank Matthew Hollis, Lavinia Singer, Kate Burton and all at Faber; Giles de la Mare and the Walter de la Mare Society; Sarah Baxter and the Society of Authors; the University of Bristol for granting me a semester of research leave; and the staff of the Senate House Library, London, the Bodleian Library in Oxford, the British Library, the Imperial War Museum, the Newberry Library in Chicago and the Harry Ransom Center, Texas.

Angela Leighton, Yui Kajita and Giles de la Mare were all kind enough to share their research with me. Stephen Cheeke, Elv Moody and David Punter gave helpful feedback on some draft commentaries. Anne Harvey and Ralph Pite enlightened me in conversation; Jane Wright and Kyra Larkin helped me with Gimmul in 'The Honey Robbers'. My intellectual debts should be clear from my endnotes, but I should also like also to note here how much I owe to Theresa Whistler's invaluable biography of Walter de la Mare, in both its published and un-truncated form.

I am grateful to Paul and Nastasha Rutman for having me to stay in Oxford. Lastly, and most importantly, I should like to thank Elisabeth Wootten for being wonderful and Lucy Wootten for being really jolly. This book is for them.

Introduction

Walter de la Mare was a magician of poetic sound. The possessor of one of the most musical ears in the history of English poetry, he had the power to write 'incantations' allowing 'Free passage to the phantoms of the mind', as T. S. Eliot puts it in his tribute 'To Walter de la Mare'. This music and magic ensured that de la Mare became one of the best-loved poets of the twentieth century and won him the admiration of W. H. Auden, Edward Thomas and Robert Frost among others.

It also won him the distrust of academic critics. For I. A. Richards and F. R. Leavis in the 1920s and 1930s, the sound of de la Mare's verse was a pernicious 'opiate', an 'enchantment', a danger to the rational reader.[1] Fifty years later, Richards apologised and hymned the 'perfection' of de la Mare's volumes *The Listeners* (1912) and *Peacock Pie* (1913).[2] This time Richards noted that their rhythms were 'haunting – not would-be, but as living presences embodying what the poems are doing'.[3] But this time was too late. Page-bound study and the academy hadn't been able to find a place for de la Mare, and having attacked and dismissed his work, soon more or less forgot about it: de la Mare's verse was for 'old-fashioned lovers of poetry' and maybe the under-twelves.

Being forgotten by the academy has its upsides, but it also has its disadvantages. In de la Mare's case, it has meant that many who understand and enjoy modern poetry either know nothing about him or have difficulty in appreciating his work. As the poet and scholar Eric Ormsby puts it in a recent essay: 'If [de la Mare's] poems sound stilted or quaintly vague, that may be because we no longer know how to read him.'[4] The easiest way to overcome such a resistance is to hear the poems read aloud. During the Second World War, Eliot, hitherto something of a de la Mare sceptic himself, was taking part in a large charitable poetry reading. He discovered, to his surprise, that it was de la Mare who 'put into his reading a more *conversational* tone' than did any other of the esteemed readers who were present.[5] Listen to other twentieth-century poets, especially the modernists, and Eliot's point is proved. Their style of recitation – and I guess the way they heard their poetry in their heads – now comes across as incredibly mannered. De la Mare, though his accent belongs to a bygone era, sounds like he's sitting in the room with you; he is reading in a way that is, as Eliot puts it, like he is 'talking to a few friends, but talking poetry'.[6] To really get de la Mare, you shouldn't be hearing his lines as an intoned singsong but in a normal prose-speaking voice, a voice which take its time and pauses at the punctuation – particularly those thoughtful, qualifying dashes. If you think his poetry sounds too artificial, you aren't reading it right.

De la Mare's poetry sounds wonderful, but it also means something, and sometimes many things at once. That old saw about poetry being understood on many levels happens to be true in his case. Moreover, because de la Mare usually prefers to hide away difficult or troubling material rather than flaunting it, there are meanings in his poems that aren't at all obvious unless they are pointed out.

De la Mare didn't object to notating poems; indeed, he was a superb writer of notes himself. Turn to his great anthologies and you'll find that not only may a note draw attention to a particular quality of sound or image or explain something of a poem's sense, it may wander off into details of folklore, history and natural history or find time to point out all manner of loosely related bits and bobs. If you want to know more not just about a poem, but what other related poem you might also like, the names of the angels, why there are no foxgloves in Shakespeare or to learn a recipe, a de la Mare note is the place to go. I'm not Walter de la Mare, but I have allowed my notes to take off into the wider world of his life and interests and included illuminating facts and by-the-ways. I have also tried to be cautious around those poems that seem to me to be crafted in a way that resists too definite an explanation and have left readers space to weigh up different accounts and find meanings of their own. The notes can be looked at as and when they might prove helpful. The poems can stand on their own, as might a straightforward *Selected*. Nevertheless, I've aimed for a book that can be read cover to cover.

The choice of poems is intended to be a showcase of what is best and most distinctive in the more than a thousand poems de la Mare published in his lifetime. Quite a number of these were first published as rhymes for children. De la Mare didn't draw a particularly firm line between his poems for adults and those he wrote for children – some of the former go down very well with younger readers, while some of the latter conceal adult themes and references – and neither do I. Indeed, when it comes to *The Listeners* and *Peacock Pie*, volumes composed

3

over the same period, I have chosen to highlight de la Mare's developing life and art by mixing the two and setting their poems in roughly chronological order.

Literary historians find it convenient to tuck de la Mare away before the First World War and the subsequent ascendancy of the modernists. But, as this book makes clear, he has a place in both the history of First World War poetry and the history of modernism. Furthermore, while his output was very uneven, he was capable of brilliant poems from the beginning of his long writing life to the end.

It is true, however, that he had golden patches. Rather than seeking to represent all parts of his career equally, I have leant towards *The Listeners* and *Peacock Pie*, but also to *Memory* (1938), and, though it was too long to include in its entirety, I have made sure the late long poem *Winged Chariot* (1951) is properly represented. There are, if you look through the *Complete Poems*, examples of satiric and social realist verse, poems addressing slums, drug addicts or the nuclear bomb; there is also some entertaining light verse. Still, de la Mare is at his strongest when he is most like de la Mare, and it is when addressing those de la Marean subjects – those deserted houses, birds, fields, flowers, children, fairies, travellers, ghosts and graves – that he makes us feel the world in a way that no other poet quite does. What's more, his poems are rarely comfort reads. They are odd and unsettling. They leave the material world and the reassuring beliefs we have about it shadowier and less certain than they found them.

De la Mare, we are always told, is a minor poet. And it is true that the word 'major' doesn't suit someone so devoted to the delicate, the unassuming and the small-scale. But he punches far above his perceived weight. Very few poets have his ability to write desert island poems. 'Autumn', 'Napoleon', 'All That's Past', 'The Listeners', 'The Song of the Mad Prince', 'Fare Well', 'The Railway Junction' and more are named by many readers as all-time favourites, but there are other, less known poems in this selection that deserve to be similarly cherished. Read de la Mare with sympathy and you may find his poems become something more important to you than words like 'major' or 'minor' can capture. They may seem indispensable.

Note on the Text

Walter de la Mare carefully saw to press the poetry volumes he published during his long life. In making the selection for this edition, I have almost exclusively followed the text of *The Complete Poems* (1969, corrections 1975), which was prepared by the Literary Trustees of Walter de la Mare. *The Complete Poems* was a major editorial undertaking: those working on it included Richard de la Mare, Giles de Mare, Leonard Clark and Dorothy Marshall. It reproduces the *Collected Poems* (1942) and *Collected Rhymes and Verses* (1944), which de la Mare approved for publication, with corrections for some minor corruptions in them. *The Complete Poems* also incorporates the volumes de la Mare published in the period between those two *Collected*s and his death, as well as numerous uncollected and unpublished poems, all of which were considered for possible inclusion in this edition, though none was in the end selected.

I have corrected one mistake in *The Complete Poems* – 'The Funeral' was, in fact, absent from the 1902 edition of *Songs of Childhood* and first included in the 1916 edition – and made two small deviations. In the case of *Winged Chariot*, I have sought to reproduce as far as possible the arrangement of text and marginalia of the 1951 edition rather than the more cramped arrangement in *The Complete Poems*, an arrangement I take to be a consequence of the dimensions of the latter volume rather than any change in authorial intention. The

7

text of 'King David' reproduced here, for reasons I explain in an endnote to my commentary, follows that of the 1913 edition of *Peacock Pie*.

Table of Dates

1873	Apr.	*b.* Walter John ('Jack') Delamare, Charlton, London
1877		family moves to 5 Bovill Terrace, Forest Hill, London
	Oct.	*d.* James Delamare (father)
1883–1990		attends St Paul's Cathedral School, London
1890		starts work at Anglo-American Oil Company
1893		meets Elfrida (Elfie) Ingpen
1895		starts to publish short stories in magazines
1899	Aug.	*m.* Elfrida Ingpen
		Mackenzie Road, Beckenham, London
1899	Oct.	*b.* Florence de la Mare (daughter)
1901	June	*b.* Richard de la Mare (son)
1902		*Songs of Childhood* (Longmans) as Walter Ramal
	Feb.	meets Henry Newbolt
1903		meets Mary Coleridge
	Aug.	*b.* Lucy ('Jinnie') de la Mare (daughter)
1904		*Henry Brocken* (Collins) (novel) as Walter J. de la Mare
1906		*Poems* (John Murray) as Walter de la Mare
	Jan.	*b.* Colin de la Mare (son)
		Samos Road, Anerley, London
1907	Mar.	meets Edward Thomas

		Worbeck Road, Anerley, London
	Aug.	*d.* Mary Coleridge
1908	July	receives one-off grant of £200; leaves Anglo-American Oil to write and review
1910		*The Return* (Edward Arnold) (novel)
		The Three Mulla-Mulgars (Duckworth) (children's novel)
1911		becomes a reader for William Heinemann and works on D. H. Lawrence's manuscripts
		14 Thornsett Road, Penge, London
	Feb.	meets Naomi Royde-Smith
1912		*The Listeners and Other Poems* (Constable)
		beginning of friendship with Forrest Reid
	Sep.	meets Rupert Brooke
	Dec.	poems included in *Georgian Poetry 1911–12* (The Poetry Bookshop)
1913	Feb.	meets Katherine Mansfield and John Middleton Murry
		Peacock Pie: A Book of Rhymes (Constable)
1914	Aug.	Britain declares war on Germany
	Nov.	appendectomy at Guy's Hospital
	Nov.	Brooke visits de la Mare in hospital
1915	Mar.	de la Mare granted a Civil List pension of £100 a year
		becomes Royal Society of Literature Chair of Fiction
		praises Brooke's war sonnets in *Times Literary Supplement*
Apr.		*d.* Rupert Brooke, Skyros

1916	Oct.	goes to America to lecture and collect post-humous award for Brooke
1917		begins war work for the Ministry of Food
	Apr.	*d.* Edward Thomas at Battle of Arras
1918		*Motley and Other Poems* (Constable)
1919	June	first performance of *Crossings*, with music by Cecil Armstrong Gibbs at the Wick School, Brighton
1920	June	tea, and last meeting, with Katherine Mansfield, Hampstead, London
1921	June	first stay with Thomas Hardy at Max Gate
		Memoirs of a Midget (Collins) (novel)
		The Veil and Other Poems
1922		*Down-Adown-Derry: A Book of Fairy Poems* (Constable)
1923	Jan.	*d.* Katherine Mansfield
		The Riddle and Other Stories (Selwyn and Blount)
		Come Hither (Constable) (anthology)
1924	Jan.	declines knighthood for first time
		Ding Dong Bell (stories)
	Dec.	Hill House, Taplow, Buckinghamshire
1925		*Broomsticks and Other Tales* (Constable) (stories for children)
1926		*The Connoisseur and Other Stories* (Collins)
1927		*Stuff and Nonsense and So On* (Constable)
		Told Again: Traditional Tales (Basil Blackwell)
		seriously ill most of year
1928	Jan.	*d.* Thomas Hardy

1929		*Stories from the Bible* (Faber)
1930		*Desert Islands* (Faber) (anthology)
		The Wind Blows Over (Faber) (stories)
1933		*The Fleeting and Other Poems* (Constable)
		The Lord Fish (Faber) (stories for children)
1935		*Early One Morning in the Spring* (Macmillan) (anthology)
1936	Jan.	meets Nathalie Saxton
		The Nap and Other Stories (1936) (Nelson)
1938		*Memory and Other Poems* (Constable)
1939		*Behold, This Dreamer!* (Faber) (anthology)
		Animal Stories (Faber) (anthology)
1940		*Pleasures and Speculations* (Faber) (essays)
		South End House, Twickenham
		Elfrida de la Mare diagnosed with Parkinson's disease
1941		*Bells and Grass: A Book of Rhymes* (Faber)
		begins friendship with physicist, Martin Johnson
1942		*The Old Lion and Other Stories* (Faber) (for children)
1943		*Love* (Faber) (anthology)
		The Magic Jacket and Other Stories (Faber) (for children)
	July	d. Elfrida de la Mare
1945		*The Burning Glass and Other Poems* (Faber)
		The Scarecrow and Other Stories (Faber) (for children)
1946		*The Traveller* (Faber) (long poem)

1946		*The Dutch Cheese* (Faber) (stories for children)
1947	Jan.	*d.* Forrest Reid
	Oct.	severe coronary thrombosis
1948		*Tribute to Walter de la Mare on his Seventy-Fifth Birthday* (Faber)
1950	Oct.	*Inward Companion and Other Poems* (Faber)
1951	Feb.	honorary degree from Oxford
		Winged Chariot (Faber) (long poem)
1952	June	Order of Merit
1953		*Private View* (Faber) (literary criticism)
		O Lovely England and Other Poems (Faber)
1955	Sep.	recording of de la Mare reading poems and in conversation ('Isn't It a Lovely Day')
		A Beginning and Other Stories (Faber)
1956	June	*d.* South End House, Twickenham

John Mouldy

I spied John Mouldy in his cellar,
Deep down twenty steps of stone;
In the dusk he sat a-smiling,
    Smiling there alone.

He read no book, he snuffed no candle;   5
The rats ran in, the rats ran out;
And far and near, the drip of water
    Went whisp'ring about.

The dusk was still, with dew a-falling,
I saw the Dog-star bleak and grim,   10
I saw a slim brown rat of Norway
    Creep over him.

I spied John Mouldy in his cellar,
Deep down twenty steps of stone;
In the dusk he sat a-smiling,   15
    Smiling there alone.

from *Songs of Childhood* (1902)

Songs of Childhood appeared in 1902 under the name Walter Ramal. The book is a successor to Robert Louis Stevenson's *A Child's Garden of Verses* (1885). Its poems bring to mind a number of nineteenth-century poets, notably Christina Rossetti, but there were some surprises too – including the shock of 'John Mouldy'.

Walter Ramal was the pen name of Walter J. de la Mare (1873–1956), who had started life with the surname Delamare and who was known to friends and family as 'Jack'. De la Mare made his living as a poorly paid clerk for the London office of J. D. Rockefeller's Standard Oil and wrote his poetry and prose in his spare time, usually after work. De la Mare had married his long-term sweetheart Elfrida Ingpen in August 1899. The couple now had two infant children, and were soon to have two more. It was, however, de la Mare's nieces and nephews who had been the first audience for the verses of *Songs of Childhood*.[1] The publishers thought that the book would be over the heads of most children, but de la Mare's rhymes expand what children's verse can be: not sentimental, as it so often was for the Victorians, nor light verse, as it is in the case of, say, the children's poems of Hilaire Belloc or T. S. Eliot, but a place where one may confront what is important, mysterious or troubling in childhood and the world outside.

In 'John Mouldy', Walter Ramal has become the poet we know as Walter de la Mare. It *is* a song of childhood. It employs the song-like oral metre we associate with verse written for children; it has a child's perspective. But that metre is supple and dextrous; that perspective on a child's fear of the dark has become one to disturb listeners of any age.

De la Mare writes in the introduction to *Animal Stories* (1939):

Many young and imaginative children are afraid of being
alone in the dark – a cupboard ajar, a creaking staircase,
an owl or a bat at the window, hobgoblins, nightmares.
A small boy with tears rolling down his cheeks sat up on
his pillow confessed to me once that he couldn't sleep for
terror because there was a bear under his bed. To console
him I assured him on my honour that there wasn't a real
bear and certainly not an uncaged bear for miles and miles
around. 'But you see, Daddie,' he replied, 'this isn't a
"*real*" bear!'[2]

The child was his own son, Richard.[3] But the truth is more
general. Moreover, not every childhood horror is imagined.
In *Early One Morning in the Spring* (1935), de la Mare notes
that while children can speak and regard death with what, to
an adult, looks like surprising blitheness,

Nevertheless, within is a self that may confront the spectre
of Death in his horror as unexpectedly as a strange dog
may be met at a turn of the street. And then it is as if the
light of life itself had gone out. [. . .] I remember – in the
company of a few other boys about ten or eleven years of
age – seeing the body of a woman who, poor hapless soul,
had been drowned in the Thames. We hung over the granite
parapet of the Embankment, the morning light reflected
from the water beating up into our faces, and stared. The

body had been secured to the stern of a police boat, and the bloated head and shoulder lolled gently in the clucking tide as the boat edged gently to and fro.[4]

But while de la Mare's prose shows a fine understanding of true and imagined childhood horror, 'John Mouldy' inhabits a realm somewhere in between the two.

Who is John Mouldy? A trick of the eye? A shape in the mould? A personification, the Jack Frost of cellar damp? An insane derelict down among the rats? Or is his smile the fixed grin of a corpse? There's no single right answer and, certainly, no answer that's a comfort. Even the conclusion that John Mouldy is but a trick of the eye is the material for a double take and a judder. Four years after *Songs of Childhood*, German psychiatrist Ernst Jentsch designated those moments when one senses something alive where no thing alive should be *unheimlich*. This is usually translated as 'uncanny', but it literally translates as 'unhomely'. According to Jentsch, the

effect of the uncanny can easily be achieved when one undertakes to reinterpret some kind of lifeless thing as part of an organic creature. [. . .] In the dark, a rafter covered with nails thus becomes the jaw of a fabulous animal, a lonely lake becomes the gigantic eye of a monster and the outline of a cloud or shadow becomes a threatening satanic face. Fantasy, which is indeed always a poet, is able now and then to conjure up the most detailed terrifying vision out of the most harmless and indifferent phenomena.[5]

In 1919 Sigmund Freud would follow Jentsch with his own explanations for such experiences, but however you wish to explain them, de la Mare is, as Peter Howarth has pointed out, the most uncanny of writers, a poet who can make us feel un-at-home in the world.[6] 'John Mouldy' doesn't just see the uncanny – it hears it too. Though 'whis'pring about' (l. 8) might mean the drips are 'whisp'ring about', as in 'running about', it could also be that they are whispering about someone or something (John Mouldy? The narrator?).

'Creep over him' (l. 12) has the same number of stresses but fewer syllables than equivalent lines elsewhere. Because of this, the line, like the rat, passes across the reader with unexpected quickness and closeness.

A 'brown rat of Norway' (l. 11) can weigh up to twice as much as a black rat. Originating, not from Norway, as was once popularly believed, but probably from China, the brown rat is believed to have arrived in England in the eighteenth century (so, long after the first arrival of the bubonic plague).[7] Its natural preference for damp habitats makes it well suited to a city's sewers, or, as here, its dripping cellars. 'The 'Dog-star' (l. 10) is Sirius, the brightest star in the night sky and a star which has since Ancient Greece been associated with the dog days of summer and hence with heat and drought. But, while this may be a summer night, the Dog-star here is 'bleak and grim'.

The Funeral

They dressed us up in black,
Susan and Tom and me;
And, walking through the fields
All beautiful to see,
With branches high in the air   5
And daisy and buttercup,
We heard the lark in the clouds, –
In black dressed up.

They took us to the graves,
Susan and Tom and me,   10
Where the long grasses grow
And the funeral tree:
We stood and watched; and the wind
Came softly out of the sky
And blew in Susan's hair,   15
As I stood close by.

Back through the fields we came,
Tom and Susan and me,
And we sat in the nursery together,
And had our tea.   20
And, looking out of the window,
I heard the thrushes sing;

But Tom fell asleep in his chair.
He was so tired, poor thing.

added to the 1916 edition of *Songs of Childhood* (1902)

If 'John Mouldy' is the most potent poem in *Songs of Childhood*, 'The Funeral' is the most sophisticated. The reason for this sophistication isn't hard to explain. *Songs of Childhood* was repeatedly revised and altered by de la Mare, and 'The Funeral' was only added to the volume in 1916, to be a reply poem to the original's 'The Christening'. By 1916, de la Mare had published two novels, *Henry Broken* (1904) and *The Return* (1910), as well as a number of short stories, and had become an adept at introducing the techniques of the fiction writer into his verse. So, though the style of 'The Funeral' maintains the simplicity of the poems in the original collection, its content is informed as much by the novels of Henry James as it is by the rhymes of *A Child's Garden of Verses*.

The poem reads like a psychological short story and plays like a movie. Point of view matters, and this point of view is used to let those descriptions of events reveal the child narrator's perceptions and emotions. Particulars that would be found in a conventional description of a funeral are omitted. We are never told who it is who is looking after these children, what the service was like or who else is in the congregation. We don't know if the children have parents. We don't even know the identity of the deceased. Yet details which would matter to the child are attended to very carefully indeed.

In the first stanza, the three children look up to branches and clouds and birds and look about to daisy and buttercup. The fields are 'All beautiful to see' (l. 4); so too are 'Susan and Tom and me' (l. 2) in their unaccustomed clothes (this may be a clue to the sex of the narrator, who, if quite a bit older than Tom, must be passing the stage where a boy would regularly be called beautiful). The children are now 'In black dressed up' (l. 8), but a brown lark seen (and heard) high up and dark against the clouds looks as if it has donned funeral clothes of its own.

In the second stanza, the children are presumably supposed to be looking downwards and watching the coffin being lowered into the earth when their eyes fix on the long grasses and the funeral tree (the yew, which partly because of its great toxicity is the most common tree in English graveyards). But if all the children's eyes wander to grass and tree as if they were still in the fields, not all the children can see the wind blowing in Susan's hair like the spirit of the departed 'as I stood close by' (l. 16) – close by Susan, but also close by the unmentioned grave.

In the third stanza, the ordering of the children's names, 'Susan and Tom and me', which we had in the first two stanzas, is changed to 'Tom and Susan and me'(l. 18). What at first seemed a mere formula now appears to recall the actual sequence in which the children were dressed up and the order in which they walked. But in this last stanza, Susan is walking more slowly, the narrator slower still, weighed down by the day's events and unvoiced grief. While the 'We' who in black heard the solitary lark in the clouds were all as one, at the end of the poem it is not 'We' who hear the thrushes sing and look out of the window, but 'I'. Tom cannot hear them because he is asleep. Whether Susan does or does not we do not know, for she and the narrator are now lost to each other.

Tom is described as a 'poor thing' (l. 24), presumably

because he is the youngest child and is tired after the day's outing, though the phrase also seems to be picking up how an adult's voice will be commiserating with the recently bereaved young boy. By falling asleep, Tom may also look like a dead child. At the start of the twentieth century, the infant mortality rate was still extremely high. Perhaps the funeral the children attend is that of another child, most likely a sibling. This might help explain why Susan and Tom and I are repeatedly joined by a fourth figure: the lark in black, the wind that comes out of the sky as if it were a soul coming down from heaven. They are, as it were, four children until the interment has laid that fourth child to rest.

Walter de la Mare's own early childhood was likewise shadowed by death. A sister, Ethel Lucy, died shortly before he was born. An uncle, who was effectively part of de la Mare's immediate family, died when he was three. Most significantly of all, de la Mare's father, James Delamare, died when Walter was four. Of his father's death de la Mare would write:

Somewhere in memory – in that densely packed yet impenetrable darkness – must lie concealed the record of my own experience when my father died in my fifth year. I can recall two sharp and meaningful glimpses of him, one of them perhaps that of bidding him goodbye; but of his death and of what immediately followed it there remains recallable not a shadow. On the other hand a sorrow was not less real because it has been forgotten; and to an observer a child may seem indifferent only because his one desire is to hide his true feelings.[1]

In de la Mare's life, as in his poetry, his father's death must have been a strong psychological prompt for all those graves and revenants, yet it is never straightforwardly recalled and expressed.

His first ten years were regarded by de la Mare as the fullest of his life, a time when his imagination and perception were more acute and alive than they could be again. While he had six siblings, including Ethel Lucy, his chief companions were the two closest to him in age: James Herbert (Bert), who was two years older than him, and Ada Mary Frances (Poppy), two years his junior. De la Mare also had a very loving relationships with his mother, a much older sister Florence (Flo) and with the family servant Martha (Pattie). On the death of de la Mare's father, the de la Mare family moved from a house in Charlton to a terraced house in the London suburb of Forest Hill. This was technically an urban address, but suburbia had not yet swallowed the countryside around London, and living on the edge of the city gave the de la Mare children access to open fields. If the pastoral is the countryside as experienced from the perspective of the city, de la Mare's was very definitely a pastoral childhood. 'The Funeral' may be pure fiction, yet in key respects the story is not far from de la Mare's own.[2]

Autumn

There is a wind where the rose was;
Cold rain where sweet grass was;
   And clouds like sheep
   Stream o'er the steep
Grey skies where the lark was.   5

Nought gold where your hair was;
Nought warm where your hand was;
   But phantom, forlorn,
   Beneath the thorn,
Your ghost where your face was.   10

Sad winds where your voice was;
Tears, tears where my heart was;
   And ever with me,
   Child, ever with me,
Silence where hope was.   15

from *Poems* (1906)

'Autumn' reads like a lament for a dead child and may indeed recall a friend from de la Mare's childhood, about which there is plenty we don't know. Still, the poem may be as much an elegy to childhood itself as to any particular childhood companion. In *Poems* (1906), 'Autumn' is placed after 'Myself', a poem which reads like a companion piece and which describes a 'garden, grey/ With mists of autumntide' wherein silently plays 'A little child like me'. 'Myself' finishes with the narrator 'alone' in the garden, 'Myself with me'. De la Mare would repeatedly return to this sense of having a double or ghost-self. For instance, the lovely children's rhyme 'The Double', from the 1922 collection *Down-Adown-Derry*, finds a young girl narrator spinning round until her dizziness creates a 'ghost' of herself that is 'a fairy child'. Martha Bremser comments that the 'de la Marean child is able not only to step out of the self and to observe his double but to step out of time, almost as though seeing the ghost of the child that will remain further on in time'.[1]

'Autumn', which originally had the title 'The Lost Playmate', dates from 1903, the year of the first publication of the long-lost works of the metaphysical poet Thomas Traherne (1636–74). Traherne, whose feelings for the transcendent and departed intensities of childhood were similar to de la Mare's, was a writer de la Mare much treasured. In Traherne's 'Shadows in the Water', the narrator recalls standing next to water in infancy:

> I fancy'd other Feet
>   Came mine to touch or meet;

> As by som[e] Puddle I did play
> Another World within it lay.[2]

The poem explores this glimpsed other world and how 'Our second Selv[e]s these shadows be'. The last stanza reads:

> Of all the Play-mates which I knew
> That here I do the Image view
> In other Selv[e]s; what can it mean?
> But that below the purling Stream
> > Som[e] unknown Joys there be
> > Laid up in Store for me;
> To which I shall, when that thin Skin
> Is broken, be admitted in.[3]

Such a sense of another world accessible to childhood and its connection both to the life before birth and the existence that may follow death, along with the attendant notion of a ghostly twin self, chimed with de la Mare's own deep sense of things. Is this the lost playmate the poem has in mind?

People's views on the metre of 'Autumn' will vary, depending on the way they choose to recite it.[4] The ambiguity of metres such as these comes from the way de la Mare is taking a cue not from literary verse but from song, especially folk song and other types of oral verse. That influence of folk song may also help explain how de la Mare's words can be reminiscent not just of a folksong-influenced composer like Ralph Vaughan Williams (1872–1958) but also singer songwriters of the English folk revival of the late 1960s, such as Nick Drake, Richard Thompson or Sandy Denny.

The most noted poet to be combining the literary and folk traditions at the time de la Mare was writing was Thomas Hardy. The American poet Horace Gregory has pointed out a Hardyesque quality to 'Autumn'.[5] Still, the Hardy poems Gregory cites as possible influences, 'The Garden Seat' and 'Transformation', were both collected some years after the publication of 'Autumn': 'Transformation' is from *Moments of Vision* (1917); the very de la Marean 'The Garden Seat', with its ghosts and repetitions, comes from *Late Lyrics and Earlier* (1922), by which time the two poets knew each other. So, if there is here a case of the influence of one poet on the other, it is the influence of de la Mare on Hardy and not the other way round.

The Birthnight: To F.

Dearest, it was a night
That in its darkness rocked Orion's stars;
A sighing wind ran faintly white
Along the willows, and the cedar boughs
Laid their wide hands in stealthy peace across   5
The starry silence of their antique moss:
No sound save rushing air
Cold, yet all sweet with Spring,
And in thy mother's arms, couched weeping there,
       Thou, lovely thing.   10

from *Poems* (1906)

The novelist William Golding (1911–93) once said 'The Birthnight' had influenced his outlook through 'its rush of continuity: there is no full stop in it. And the way it articulates itself in a single breath of feeling and exclamation' and that he had attempted to 'do the same, in a novel'.[1]

This is literally and figuratively a poem of breath. The Latin word for breath, but also for life, soul or spirit is 'anima'. From it we get the word 'animism', the belief system that gives souls to non-human things including plants, animals and the weather. Poets often animate the world in their tropes, but they don't usually mean us to take the idea seriously. De la Mare, on the other hand, imparts an amazed earnestness to his depiction of the life of wind, trees and stars. It was a night which 'rocked Orion's stars' (l. 2) – 'rocked' because the universe seemed changed and also because it was a night that rocked the stars to sleep as if they were a newborn babe. 'A sighing wind ran faintly white' (l. 3) may simply indicate the appearance of willow leaves turning in the wind or may, as Golding noted, be observing how 'on a very dark night a light wind [. . .] can give the strange effect of diminishing the darkness'.[2] This wind not only sighs but runs, then, while the no-less-alive-but-reverent cedar boughs lay 'their wide hands in stealthy peace' (l. 5). At the end, couched tenderly in her last small line, is the baby herself. And, as Eric Ormsby observes, with the description of her as 'Thou, lovely thing' (l. 10), the child herself becomes a 'thing amongst things, and in this, like the stars and the wind, the willows and the mosses.'[3]

The cause of this great soul-seeing in the wide world was Florence de la Mare, born not in spring but on 21 October

1899.[4] Florence was the de la Mares' first child and was to be followed by Richard in 1901, Jinnie in 1903 and Colin in 1906. De la Mare had been reluctant to wed Elfrida, who was ten years his senior, prior to the pregnancy, but he was to prove a devoted father as well as a very hands-on one – there can't have been many men born in 1873 who were, as de la Mare was, quite comfortable with changing a nappy.

You wouldn't guess it from 'The Birthnight' any more than you would guess that this was a metaphorical spring (l. 8) rather than a literal one, but Florence was born in a rented villa in the South London suburb of Beckenham. The 'To F.' of the title was added, presumably with Florence's approval, when the poem appeared in *Collected Poems 1901–18*. Still, the poem always was very much *to* Florence rather than simply about her. It is an answer to the question, 'Daddy, what was it like, the night when I was born?'

Napoleon

'What is the world, O soldiers?
    It is I:
I, this incessant snow,
    This northern sky;
Soldiers, this solitude   5
    Through which we go
        Is I.'

from *Poems* (1906)

The poem's speaker is the Napoleon of the Russian campaign of 1812, a campaign in which, according to the historian Adam Zamoyski, between 'the end of June 1812 and the end of February 1813, about a million people died, fairly equally divided between two sides'.[1] Of these, '400,000 French and allied troops' perished, 'less than a quarter of them in battle'.[2]

As the poetry-loving military commander and Viceroy of India, Field Marshal Earl Wavell, writes in his anthology *Other Men's Flowers*: 'De la Mare's comment on Napoleon's monstrous egotism . . . may have been inspired by the well-known conclusion of the letter in which Napoleon recorded the destruction of his army in 1812 –"The Emperor is in excellent health".'[3] This was the 29th Bulletin of the Grande Armée, dated 3 December but dictated on the fifth. Perhaps the final remark was there 'to reassure his subjects that he was alive and well', as Philip G. Dwyer and Peter McPhee suggest, but the rest of the letter, in which Napoleon blames everyone and everything for the defeat except himself, is scarcely less egotistical in tone.[4] De la Mare may also have in mind Napoleon's remarks to Prince Klemens von Metternich in Dresden the following year:

> I may defy man, but not the elements; the cold has ruined me. In one night I lost thirty thousand horses. I have lost everything, except honour and the consciousness of what I owe to a brave people who, after such enormous misfortunes, have given me fresh proofs of their devotion and their conviction that I alone can rule them.[5]

Napoleon is also reported to have said on this occasion: 'a man such as I does not concern himself much about the lives of a million men' (or words to that effect: Metternich indicates Napoleon's actual language was too vulgar to be written down).[6]

A further possible prompt for the 'It is I' of de la Mare's poem can be found in the notes to his 1923 anthology *Come Hither*, where he quotes a passage from a letter written by Amelia Opie from Paris to a friend in England in 1802:

Just before the review was expected to begin, we saw several officers in gorgeous uniforms ascend the stairs, one of whom, whose helmet seemed entirely of gold, was, as I was told, [Napoleon's stepson] Eugène de Beauharnais. A few minutes afterwards there was a rush of officers down the stairs, and amongst them I saw a short, pale man, with his hat in his hand . . . but, though my friend said in a whisper, "*C'est lui*," ['It is he'] I did not comprehend that I beheld Buonaparte, till I saw him stand alone at the gate. [. . .]

At length the review ended; too soon for me. The Consul sprang from his horse – we threw open our door again, and, as he slowly reascended the stairs, we saw him very near us, and in full face again, while his bright, restless, expressive, and, as we fancied, dark blue eyes, beaming from under long black eyelashes, glowed over us with a scrutinising but complacent look . . .

I could not speak; I had worked myself up to all my former enthusiasm for Buonaparte; and my frame still shook with the excitement I had undergone.[7]

De la Mare comments that, 'as to those "dark blue eyes"', 'Amelia Opie was right in using the word "fancied", as there seems little doubt that Napoleon's eyes were a light blue grey – "*gris bleu*".'[8] De la Mare then heads off into a digression on the subject of eyes and eye colour.

The odd way that the 'I' of Napoleon seems to be connected in de la Mare's mind to the eyes of Napoleon surfaces again in his 1930 extended essay-cum-anthology *Desert Islands* (1930), where he recalls a dream in which he witnessed the exhumation of Napoleon:

The attenuated body – that of the young Napoleon, not the hermit of St Helena – was clothed to the feet in a long dark military coat, stained with damp and mould. I recall no buttons on the breast, or they were too much tarnished to be conspicuous. On the head was a three-cornered hat. The lower part of the ashy face beneath the ivory brows was narrowed and fallen in under the high cheek bones; and the two eyes in that head gazed out at me with a marvellous effulgence. I gazed back – those eyes that in life few men had ever dared to meet – then turned my head and spoke in astonishment to those who stood near me but whom I could not see, and said, 'Then his eyes were not blue, or grey-blue? They are bright brown.'

Then I turned again and met that intense yet unspeculating gaze once more. 'No, not brown,' I added in a low voice, and as if to myself, 'orange-brown'. But this too was inaccurate; flat, wide, unblinking, intent, they were far more red than orange – a clear lively red.

And there passed through my mind as I continued to
meet and bandy thoughts with them, vague tumultuous
remembrances of this supreme egoist and man of genius,
and of the glory that was gone. . . .

In searching afterwards for some germ of this dream, I
recalled at once an unusually intelligent black cat, once
an admired pet, named Caesar. It died some months ago,
miserably shrunken. [. . .] A few hours before it died the
colour of its eyes became changed to a curiously bright
strange green. And now, as I look back, these eyes too had
looked out at me – as I myself looked down in horror at
the poor dying creature – like those of the dead Napoleon;
as if there were some secret between us, as if in some
way I shared the responsibility, the blame for what had
passed.[9]

'Napoleon' is only seven lines on a subject that seems suited
to the epic, and it could in theory have been even shorter.
Joe Griffiths points out that it would be possible to reset the
poem as three lines: two pentameter lines and an alexandrine.
However, in creating the stanza form we have here, de la
Mare is able perfectly to match his subject: lines that trudge
through the vastness repeatedly contract back to the man who
has willed that trudge, the repeated 'I' of Napoleon.[10]

Longlegs

Longlegs – he yelled 'Coo-ee!'
  And all across the combe
Shrill and shrill it rang – rang through
  The clear green gloom.
Fairies there were a-spinning,   5
  And a white tree-maid
Lifted her eyes, and listened
  In her rain-sweet glade.
Bunnie to bunnie stamped; old Wat
  Chin-deep in bracken sate;   10
A throstle piped, 'I'm by, I'm by!'
  Clear to his timid mate.
And there was Longlegs straddling,
  And hearkening was he,
To distant Echo thrilling back   15
  A thin 'Coo-ee!'

from *Peacock Pie: A Book of Rhymes* (1913)

Longlegs yells high and loud enough, and listens hard enough, to hear Echo return his call back across the combe, a 'combe' (l. 2) being a steep, narrow valley without running water at the bottom. With Longlegs' voice coming from one side and then the other, it is as if his long legs are 'straddling' (l. 13) the gulf.

As it goes from one side to another, the cry makes little echoes on its way: 'Shrill and shrill', 'rang – rang' (l. 3), 'Bunnie to bunnie' (l. 9), 'I'm by, I'm by!' (l. 11). Some of these little echoes are also the sounds of one animal to another: the stamping of bunny to bunny is a warning signal; a throstle (a thrush) is calling to his 'timid mate'. 'Longlegs', or to give him his full title 'Daddy Longlegs', is the dialect name for a crane-fly. 'Wat' is a dialect nickname for a hare. The name appears in a passage from Shakespeare's *Venus and Adonis*, which is quoted by de la Mare in *Come Hither*.[1]

At the end of the rhyme, Echo's voice is literally 'thrilling' (l. 15): it is piercing or penetrating. It helps to 'coo-ee' high as well as loud, if you want your call to carry. Longlegs is male, but assuming the sound coming back is a literal echo, it would now sound more female than male: Longlegs has been transformed into Echo. De la Mare doesn't make much use of classical mythology, but his capitalisation of Echo inevitably recalls the story of Echo, found in Book III of Ovid's *Metamorphoses*, in which Echo is cursed by Juno, her voice henceforth being a fainter repetition of another's. Following this, Echo then falls in love with Narcissus, who rejects her advances. Venus answers Echo's prayers by rendering her invisible.

When it appeared again in de la Mare's 1922 collection of fairy poems, *Down-Adown-Derry*, 'Longlegs' was given the dedication 'To E.T.'.[2] E.T. was Edward Thomas (1878–1917). In the years before the First World War, Thomas was a prolific book reviewer, country writer and general man of letters. Though Helen Thomas, his wife, was to remember 'pouncing on *Poems of Childhood* [sic] by de la Mare' while looking through the many books her husband had to review, Thomas had reviewed *Songs of Childhood* with little praise.[3] When he came to review *Poems* (1906), he was far more positive about the new poems, but also the old, which he now found the work of a man 'whose every verse was his own, just as every nightingale's egg is olive'.[4]

An acquaintance was struck up after Thomas wrote to de la Mare asking to anthologise a poem. The two arranged to meet in a Mecca café in St George's Yard in London. While waiting, de la Mare heard 'presently out of a neighbouring court echoed that peculiarly leisurely footfall'.[5] In this urban setting, the long-limbed, country-dwelling Thomas seemed like Gulliver in Lilliput. He and de la Mare then sat and talked 'until the tactful waitresses piled chairs on the marble-topped tables around us as a tacit hint that we might outstay our welcome'.[6]

Not only would de la Mare and Thomas go on to meet most weeks in London, often in the company of other literary friends such as Ralph Hodgson (1871–1962), W. H. Davies (1871–1940), Edward Garnett (1868–1937) and John Freeman (1880–1929), Thomas also began inviting de la Mare to stay with him in Hampshire, and by 1909 the Thomas and de la Mare families were sharing their summer holidays.[7] The two writers would regularly comment on one another's work, and they also promoted one another in print. Thomas's glowing reviews of *The Listeners* and *Peacock Pie*, many of whose poems he had looked at and commented upon over the preceding six years and helped to sort into their respective volumes, undoubtedly helped make de la Mare into a popular writer. But the admiration was genuine. Thomas told Eleanor Farjeon that in all the hundreds of books he had reviewed over the years, *Peacock Pie* was, along with Robert Frost's *North of Boston*, the only pure gold he ever unearthed.[8]

There are numerous reminiscences of de la Mare's work in the poems Thomas would produce after the end of 1914, when he turned to writing verse, many of which are documented by Judy Kendall in her book *Edward Thomas's Poets*. Kendall also points out that, though Thomas never wrote a poem which explicitly addressed de la Mare, his poem 'The Sun Used to Shine', while principally addressing itself to Thomas's friendship with the American poet Robert Frost (1874–1963), echoes Thomas's story 'The Stile', from *Light and Twilight* (1911).[9] A letter from Helen Thomas to de la Mare declares: 'Edward loved you more than any man & his loveliest of all his essays "The Stile" enshrines his feeling for you.'[10] Helen Thomas had reason to write as she did: her letter, though undated, was clearly composed after she had fallen out with Frost. Nevertheless, 'The Stile' depicts not just a strong friendship, but one whose conversation could be of a particular sort. At one point in the story, Thomas writes:

We had been talking easily and warmly together, in such a way that there was no knowing what any one thought, because we were in electrical contact and each leapt to complete the other's words, just as if some poet had chosen to use the form of an eclogue and had made us the two shepherds who were to utter his mind through our dialogue.[11]

The echoes and similarities in the work of the two writers can read like a straightforward continuing of their form of conversation.

'Longlegs' seems to have been inspired by a stay with the Thomases at their house in Wick Green in the spring of 1910. On 8 May Thomas was signing himself 'Longlegs' in a letter to de la Mare, and I would imagine de la Mare wrote the poem either during his stay or in a thank-you letter – it is impossible be sure because Thomas appears to have burned all the letters he still had from de la Mare in a great bonfire of private correspondence made before he went to the Front in 1917.[12] Helen Thomas recalls how she and Edward would call 'coo-ee' to their children across the combe, in order to cheer them up on their way home from school.[13] Invisible through the foliage, and still half an hour from their destination, the children would 'coo-ee' back.

Thomas's *In Pursuit of Spring* recalls an incident cycling over Salisbury Plain:

A motor car overtook me in the village, scattering a group of boys.

'Look out!' cried one, and as the thing passed by, turned to the next boy with, 'There's a fine motor; worth more than you are; cost a lot of money.'

Is this not the awakening of England? At least, it is truth. One pink foxy boy laughed in my face as if there had been iron bars or a wall of plate glass dividing us; another waited till I had started, to hail me –

'Longlegs'.[14]

The nickname suited Thomas: he was a great walker and considerably taller than the more sedentary de la Mare. The poet–critic Angela Leighton points out that, as Wat is short for Walter, Wat the hare may be a jokey self-portrait of the ever-listening de la Mare.[15] The inspiration for the white tree-maid is, I assume, Helen Thomas.

King David

King David was a sorrowful man:
    No cause for his sorrow had he:
And he called for the music of a hundred harps,
    To ease his melancholy.

They played till they all fell silent: 5
    Played – and play sweet did they;
But the sorrow that haunted the heart of King David
    They could not charm away.

He rose; and in his garden
    Walked by the moon alone.   10
A nightingale in a cypress-tree
    Jargoned on and on.

King David lifted his sad eyes
    Into the dark-boughed tree –
'Tell me, thou little bird that singest,   15
    Who taught my grief to thee?'

But the bird in no wise heeded;
    And the king in the cool of the moon
Hearkened to the nightingale's sorrowfulness,
    Till all his own was gone.   20

from *Peacock Pie: A Book of Rhymes* (1913)

'Old King Cole' has been transformed, and in place of the merry old soul of the nursery rhyme, we have a melancholy one: King David, the psalmist of the Old Testament. David used his harp to heal the mental distress of others. In 1 Samuel 16:23 we learn: 'And it came to pass, when the *evil* spirit from God was upon Saul, that David took an harp and played with his hand; so Saul was refreshed and was well, and the evil spirit departed from him.' But here it is David who is cast down. Jeremy Dibble suggests that this is due to David's guilt over his adultery with Bathsheba and the death of Uriel and his grief over the death of his son Absalom.[1] But while the figure of King David can't help but bring such sadnesses to mind, the poem explicitly says that the melancholy it describes has no cause.

There is no single passage in the Bible that closely matches the story told in 'King David', and, as a matter of fact, there are no nightingales (l. 11) in the Bible. King David, garden and nightingales *are* all mentioned together in *The Conference of the Birds* by the medieval Persian poet Farid ud-din Attar, Attar of Nishapur, in which the nightingale sings like David in 'love's garden'.[2] But the lines where they come together most strongly are omitted from the abridged translation by Edward Fitzgerald, the only English translation readily available to de la Mare at the time of *Peacock Pie*, so this may be a coincidence. Less likely to be a coincidence are the poem's resemblances to Hans Christian's Andersen's tale 'The Nightingale' and to Keats's 'Ode on Melancholy' and 'Ode to a Nightingale'.

De la Mare could himself be melancholic, and he strongly

valued the transcendent effect of birdsong. Nevertheless, 'King David' may have been less inspired by his own experience than that of the nightingale-loving Edward Thomas. When Thomas wrote to de la Mare in June 1909, commenting on a large batch of poems sent him by his friend, 'King David' was one of only four Thomas did *not* like.[3] The chief objection may have been stylistic – the archaism of some of the language, though entirely fitted to the poem's theme, may not have been to Thomas's taste, but, since Thomas's 'melancholy' was what we would term 'clinical depression', and since he experienced the songs of nightingales as profound comfort rather than cure, Thomas may also have felt the experience of King David did not ring quite true.[4,5]

'King David' will be known to many from its 1919 setting by the composer Herbert Howells (1892–1983). Howells, who first met de la Mare when he was seventeen or eighteen, was to set a number of de la Mare poems to music but professed himself 'prouder to have written *King David* than almost anything else of mine'. De la Mare, for his part, appears to have thought the setting definitive, telling Howells he did not want anyone else to set the poem.[6] De la Mare's talent for the compressed lyric narrative and for the emotional development within it must also have proved very attractive to Howells, demanding as it does to be matched in the melodic and harmonic development of the setting. In the case of 'King David', that journey not only includes harps and nightingale but the movement from a melancholic E flat minor to a conclusion in E major that is, as the Howells scholar Christopher Palmer points out, the Edenic key of Schubert and Delius. In this, Howells was showing a profound rapport not just with the explicit narrative of the poem but with the connection between Edenic sound and birdsong to be found elsewhere in de la Mare's work.[7] Howells told Christopher Palmer: 'I always enjoyed talking music to de la Mare; he was one of the few poets I've known who really *understood* music – one always felt he was on one's wavelength, for instance his concept of "rhythm" was identical with one's own.'[8]

De la Mare's poems, especially those from *Peacock Pie*, proved to be great favourites with a host of other composers besides Howells, including: Benjamin Britten (1913–76), Arthur Bliss (1891–1975), Ivor Gurney (1890–1937) and Cecil Armstrong Gibbs (1889–1960). Richard Stokes's statement in the *Penguin Book of English Song* that there have been more settings of de la Mare poems than any other English poet can't be far wide of the mark.[9] Colin Scott-Sutherland, citing Stephen Banfield's two-volume work *Sensibility and the English Song*, finds that, as of 1985, there were 126 settings of de la Mare's poems, 'a total only exceeded by settings of Shakespeare (150) and of Housman (162)'.[10] But this is a very conservative count. In her bibliography of *Solo Song Settings of the Poetry of Walter de la Mare*, Adèle L. Paxton discovers nearly 800 solo settings, so the total number of settings will be higher still.[11]

l. 11. 'cypress-tree' is a tree that has long been associated with death; it is famously the coffin wood of 'Come away, come away, death,/ And in sad cypress let me be laid' in

Shakespeare's *Twelfth Night* (Act II, Sc. 4) where it is sung by the melancholic clown, Feste.

l. 12. 'Jargoned' is used in its Middle English sense of 'twittering' or 'chattering'.

An Epitaph

Here lies a most beautiful lady,
Light of step and heart was she;
I think she was the most beautiful lady
That ever was in the West Country.

But beauty vanishes; beauty passes;   5
However rare – rare it be;
And when I crumble, who will remember
This lady of the West Country?

from *The Listeners and Other Poems* (1912)

A choral scholarship gave de la Mare the education his family could not afford, at St Paul's School in London, where he studied until he had to leave and find work at sixteen. Long hours in the cathedral and its churchyard fostered a fondness for epitaphs. Later, the epitaphs of Robert Herrick (1591–1674) and essays and poems by William Wordsworth (1770–1850) revealed how the epitaph could be a species of literature. This taste for epitaphs was shared with Edward Thomas, who had also attended St Paul's, and both writers combed churchyards for choice examples, some of which they would place in their anthologies. Indeed, graveyards were a particular bond. When visiting Dunwich Graveyard when it was tumbling into the sea, Thomas procured de la Mare a skull, which de la Mare christened 'Moses' and kept in a Viennese cake box.[1]

Writers of actual epitaphs will occasionally have literary pretensions. Still, what we find in churchyards, church memorials and cemeteries are, in essence, folk rhymes, and de la Mare's and Thomas's interest in them, and de la Mare's interest in the virtues of good 'doggerel', is of a piece with their interest in popular art, such as folk song, folk rhymes and folk tales. As W. B. Yeats remarked of 'An Epitaph': 'There is not an original sentence in this poem, yet it will live for centuries.'[2]

For such a short poem, there is much repetition and near repetition; and yet the poem never says the same thing twice. 'Here lies a most beautiful lady' (l. 1) is a polite compliment to the deceased; 'I think she was the most beautiful lady/ That ever was in the West Country' (ll. 3–4) feels personal and heartfelt. In the case of 'Beauty vanishes' and 'beauty

54

passes' (l. 5), if, as it seems, this lady died young, her beauty will have vanished for the beholder; had she lived, it would have passed. The repetition of 'rare', divided by one of de la Mare's dashes, is an emotional one, a long moment to dwell on what has passed; it also makes us wonder, at least in the second instance, whether 'rare' may be used to mean rarely occurring as well as of rare quality.

Theresa Whistler identifies Naomi Royde-Smith (see '"The Hawthorn Hath a Deathly Smell"') as the 'beautiful lady' and, on that basis, Wales as the West Country.[3] De la Mare does seem to have indicated to Royde-Smith that she inspired 'An Epitaph' when, on 22 January 1912, he sent her a copy of the poem.[4] However, since a poem called an 'An Epitaph' is praised by Thomas in his letter to de la Mare of 4 November 1908, and since de la Mare was not to meet Royde-Smith until the spring of 1911, it is safer to conclude either that de la Mare had someone else in mind – he was close to Ella Coltman, who at least lived in the right part of the world – or that the lady is as fictitious as her epitaph.

Nobody Knows

Often I've heard the Wind sigh
  By the ivied orchard wall,
Over the leaves in the dark night,
  Breathe a sighing call,
And faint away in the silence,   5
  While I, in my bed,
Wondered, 'twixt dreaming and waking,
    What it said.

Nobody knows what the Wind is,
  Under the height of the sky,   10
Where the hosts of the stars keep far away house
  And its wave sweeps by –
Just a great wave of the air,
  Tossing the leaves in its sea,
And foaming under the eaves of the roof   15
    That covers me.

And so we live under deep water,
  All of us, beasts and men,
And our bodies are buried down under the sand,
  When we go again;   20
And leave, like the fishes, our shells,
  And float on the Wind and away,

To where, o'er the marvellous tides of the air,
    Burns day.

from *Peacock Pie*: *A Book of Rhymes* (1913)

Any child who can listen to it must know the wind in the leaves may have the sound of the sea. In this poem, this discovery becomes a mystical insight. The whole world turns strange as we sense what it is that nobody knows: the secrets discovered by those who have no body to weigh them down.

In the first verse, the narrator, at home in bed and half-awake, listens to the sound of the wind rustling the ivy by the orchard wall. It speaks a language one could maybe under-stand if one listened aright, and it makes a 'call' (l. 4). Whom it calls or what it signifies we are not told – as with the 'sighing wind' of 'The Birthnight', the depiction of the sighing, call-ing wind seems to be more of a literal apprehension of spirit, perhaps the Holy Spirit, but the rest of the rhyme may be taken as the narrator's best guess.

It is the 'hosts of the stars' (l. 11), not 'the host': not many stars but stars like distant, lit houses by the seashore, whose hosts await their coming guests. The narrator, though not at home in house or world, knows that beyond the surface of this sea we call the wind and air there might be a true home-coming. In the third verse, the condition of all creatures of the earth has become that of the creatures of the sea. The phrase 'like the fishes' (l. 21) doesn't refer to fishes having shells, but to the bodies of 'beasts and men' (l. 18) as being like shells which when shed at the point of death may allow souls to swim through the air in the way that fishes swim through water, the earth of the grave now being like the sand on the sea floor. Since air is now like water, men may swim up to the surface and the true light which lies beyond. The thought that we do not see the real sun and that we only see it as if we were under water is akin to Platonic and Neoplatonic thinking, but also in accord with Christian doctrine: ' For now we see through a glass, darkly; but then face to face: now I know in part; but then shall I know even as also I am known', 1 Corinthians, 13:12. The depiction of the wind here also feels biblical, bringing to mind verses including John 3:8: 'The wind bloweth where it listeth, and thou hearest the sound thereof, but canst not tell whence it cometh, and whither it goeth: so is every one that is born of the Spirit.'

The verse form of 'Nobody Knows' looks and sounds more regular than it is, de la Mare taking advantage of the metrical freedoms he allows himself, particularly in his children's verse. Hear how the penultimate line of the second verse swells to match the expansiveness of the narrator's contemplation of the wind as the sea, before covering 'me' in that verse's small, but not quite so small, last line. Then hear how at the very end of the poem the two stresses of 'Burns day' (l. 24) break through the surface.

The Bells

Shadow and light both strove to be
The eight bell-ringers' company,
As with his gliding rope in hand,
Counting his changes, each did stand;
While rang and trembled every stone,   5
To music by the bell-mouths blown:
Till the bright clouds that towered on high
Seemed to re-echo cry with cry.
Still swang the clappers to and fro,
When, in the far-spread fields below,   10
I saw a ploughman with his team
Lift to the bells and fix on them
His distant eyes, as if he would
Drink in the utmost sound he could;
While near him sat his children three,   15
And in the green grass placidly
Played undistracted on: as if
What music earthly bells might give
Could only faintly stir their dream,
And stillness make more lovely seem.   20
Soon night hid horses, children, all,
In sleep deep and ambrosial.
Yet, yet, it seemed, from star to star,
Welling now near, now faint and far,

Those echoing bells rang on in dream,   25
And stillness made even lovelier seem.

from *The Listeners and Other Poems* (1912)

Most English church bells are rung and not chimed. Each bell-ringer pulls on a rope, which tips the bell and swings the clapper to make the sound. The bell-ringers in this poem are 'change ringing': they are ringing the bells in a particular sequence, and because they are 'method ringers' who agree in advance on a 'method' that will generate the various sequences in which the bells are to be rung rather than listening to them being called out, each is 'counting his changes' (l. 4).

The bell-ringers can't actually see the bells above their heads, only the bell ropes gliding through their hands, and, having a ceiling or two above them cushioning the sound, do not hear them at their loudest. The poem thus takes a true observation – that the sound of the bells will be louder at a certain distance from the bell tower than it is to the bell-ringers within it – and magnifies it hugely. The power of the bells carries on increasing, not just over distance but over time, becoming strongest after their sound has passed into silence, night and dream.

What is described in the poem is akin to what is known as the Romantic 'after-image'. In 'I Wandered Lonely as a Cloud', for instance, William Wordsworth's pleasure in the daffodils is not just in the moment he first sees them, but when, later on his couch: 'They flash upon that inward eye/ Which is the bliss of solitude'.[1] Similarly, after Wordsworth's ears have ceased to hear the song of the 'The Solitary Reaper', he finds that as he mounts up the hill: 'The music in my heart I bore,/ Long after it was heard no more.'[2] As Geoffrey Hartman points out, the Wordsworthian 'after-image or echo may occur at a distance from the original experience, and still be part of it', and the passage of time becomes of little consequence.[3] 'After-image' is a term that de la Mare uses himself. In his story 'The Green Room', de la Mare writes of a face remembered from a photograph reappearing to haunt the protagonist 'as unembodied an object as the after-image of a flower'.[4] In 'The Bells', the after-image does not merely exist undiminished at a distance – that distance allows it to become ever more potent.

As the poem moves out in space and in distance from the bells, different listeners perceive the sound in their different ways. The ploughman seems to hear them as a call to prayer, or at least as heavenly peals far from soil and toil. His children, more attuned to the less earthly bells their father pines for, play on regardless. Come nightfall, the narrator feels the bells' echo ring on into silence and a dreaming that is like the refrain of the seeming and dreaming experienced by the children.

It is common to think of shadows and echoes, dreams and mental seemings as diminishments of the real. In Plato's *The Republic*, the parable of a firelit cave purports to reveal how most inhabit a world of shadows, and that only the philosopher can escape to truth and light and then report back. It is a conception that has little time for poetry – the art's status as an imitation of an imitation, a shadow of a shadow, is one of the reasons the poets are thrown out of the Republic. Dreams have been looked on in much the same way, and Shakespeare conjures with such questions in *A Midsummer Night's Dream*. De la Mare, however, turns the whole Platonic scheme on its head. Each step away from the originating 'real sound' is a step towards rich silence and darkness that imagines sights it can no longer see and sound it can no longer hear. The thing itself is less to be valued than the effect it produces, the object is inferior to the shadow and the sound is less than its echo will be.

The Listeners

'Is there anybody there?' said the Traveller,
   Knocking on the moonlit door;
And his horse in the silence champed the grasses
   Of the forest's ferny floor:
And a bird flew up out of the turret,   5
   Above the Traveller's head:
And he smote upon the door again a second time;
   'Is there anybody there?' he said.
But no one descended to the Traveller;
   No head from the leaf-fringed sill   10
Leaned over and looked into his grey eyes,
   Where he stood perplexed and still.
But only a host of phantom listeners
   That dwelt in the lone house then
Stood listening in the quiet of the moonlight   15
   To that voice from the world of men:
Stood thronging the faint moonbeams on the dark stair,
   That goes down to the empty hall,
Hearkening in an air stirred and shaken
   By the lonely Traveller's call.   20
And he felt in his heart their strangeness,
   Their stillness answering his cry,
While his horse moved, cropping the dark turf,
   'Neath the starred and leafy sky;
For he suddenly smote on the door, even   25

Louder, and lifted his head: –
'Tell them I came, and no one answered,
    That I kept my word,' he said.
Never the least stir made the listeners,
    Though every word he spake   30
Fell echoing through the shadowiness of the still house
    From the one man left awake:
Ay, they heard his foot upon the stirrup,
    And the sound of iron on stone,
And how the silence surged softly backward,   35
    When the plunging hoofs were gone.

from *The Listeners and Other Poems* (1912)

The Traveller knocks at a moonlit door to ask, 'Is there anybody there?' His horse grazes. They have come to a 'lone house' (l. 14), a solitary house but also a lonely one, with a turret from which a bird then flies out (l. 5), presumably disturbed by the knock. The Traveller then knocks at the door again, firmly and loudly ('smote' (l. 7)) repeating his question. While 'no one' descends to the Traveller and 'no head' (l. 10) leans out of the 'leaf-fringed' window, this no one and this no head behave as if they are someones: one of them comes down the stairs to the Traveller; the other leans out of the window and looks into the Traveller's grey eyes. They are, as it were, answering the Traveller's call. To confirm the haunting, we are told how 'a host of phantom listeners' dwelled in the 'lone house then' (l. 14). The 'then' might indicate either that the listeners used to dwell there and now no longer do or that they only dwelt there for that brief moment, summoned by the Traveller's knock and cry. These listeners listen 'in the quiet of the moonlight/ To that voice from the world of men' (ll. 15–16) and crowd the dark stairs of an empty hall. If the Traveller has come from the world of men, he has arrived at a house that seems to be built beyond that world. Since 'phantom' tends to be a synonym for 'ghost', the obvious conclusion would be that this is either a haunted house or a place in the afterlife. And yet, since the word 'phantom' has traditionally been used to indicate delusions or dream images, it is also possible to think of these listeners as projections from the mind of the Traveller, beings not from the world of men because they are not really there at all. Ghosts or figments, the Traveller's knock *is* answered by the Listeners, at least after a fashion: it is '*their* strangeness,/ *Their* stillness answering his cry' (ll. 21–2) (my italics).

The horse carries on eating and the Traveller smites the door a third time. Rather than asking his question again, he makes a statement: 'Tell them I came, and no one answered,/ That I kept my word' (ll. 27–8). The Traveller needs whomever or whatever he thinks might be listening or capable of answering the door to pass on a message, to tell an unspecified 'them' that he came and that he kept his word. From this, we can infer both some promise made before the poem begins and that it is the Traveller's coming to the house that is the act by which his word is kept. And yet *has* he kept his word? He certainly does not keep his *words*: each one of them falls 'echoing through the shadowiness of the still house' (l. 31); if they are kept by anyone it is the listeners rather than 'the one man left awake' (l. 32) – is this a house of sleep, or is 'awake' used euphemistically, making this a house of death? The Traveller, who must be 'the one man' (l. 32), then rides off. We are told that the listeners heard him and that a water-like silence 'surged softly backward' (l. 35) when the 'plunging' (l. 36) (literally 'thrusting down', but also figuratively diving down into the silence) 'hoofs were gone' (l. 36).

The poem, in my account at least, leaves certain key questions unanswered, or at least uncertain. This quality of indefiniteness is part of the poem's great allure. In a lecture about how to teach and how not to teach poetry, and in particular 'The Listeners', to children, Michael Rosen admits, 'I have never known who the Traveller and the listeners are, and I suspect I never will', before going on to say: 'I also think that its unknowability might be what's important or interesting about it.'[1] Not only is this a poem with the glamour of mystery, it has the power to raise in us greater and more troubling feelings as to our place in the world and our uncertainties.

This does not mean, of course, that there isn't a part of us that is interested in hearing a definite answer. In his lifetime, many people asked de la Mare to supply one. His preferred response seems to have been that which he gave in his final interview, with Boris Ford: yes, he knew what he meant in the poem, but that the 'meaning's in the poem itself, or it's nowhere. And if it's not in the poem, then it's certainly not worth bothering about.'[2] The poet's son Richard de la Mare recalled that in order to deal with the many enquiries about the poem's meaning, his father 'made up a particular explanation, but I think he was amused at the necessity for it'.[3] This was probably the story given to the critic F. L. Lucas, who writes in his 1948 study *The Decline and Fall of the Romantic Ideal*: 'it should be remembered – I have it on the poet's authority – that the Traveller is himself the ghost'.[4] Since the explanation makes the one person in the poem you thought *wasn't* a ghost into one, the answer seems almost too good to be true. Still, de la Mare does proffer a similar solution to his correspondent J. G. Syme on 7 February 1944, even if he then more or less takes it away again:

As to 'The Listeners' – I have frequently been asked to expound its meaning and in reply have usually suggested that the very kind enquirer should keep to any meaning he may have been able to find in it. As Lewis Carroll once said [. . .] 'Since words mean more than one means when one uses them, I shall be very pleased to accept whatever meanings you may have discovered' in mine [. . .] Moreover (quite between ourselves of course!), I am now a little vague concerning what was the intended meaning of those particular lines. Its rudiments, I think, were that the Traveller is a reincarnation revisiting the world beneath the glimpses of the moon, and there asking the same old unanswerable questions of the Listeners – only conceived but never embodied, who forever frequent, it would seem, this earthly existence, but then are even these rudiments definable – from the poem? Every poem, of course, to its last syllable *is* its meaning; to attempt any paraphrase of the poem is in some degree to change that meaning and its effect on the imagination, and often disastrously. What the poem (or even a letter for that matter) means is inherent in its terms and (however wide their implications may be) that meaning is nothing less and nothing different.[5]

The idea that the Traveller was envisioned as being a revenant, at some point in the poem's composition if not necessarily in the final drafting, is given credence by the corrected page proofs of 'The Listeners' in which the line 'Stood listening in the quiet of the moonlight' (l. 15) is an alteration of what had been 'Stood listening awisp in the moonlight'.[6] Full-blooded people aren't usually 'awisp'.

Hints, most notably that conspicuous capital T given to the Traveller, encourage us to read 'The Listeners' as an allegory. And one can offer a fairly convincing allegorical account of the poem: the bird flying from the turret could be interpreted as the departing soul, the horse as, perhaps, the unquestioning appetitive spirit of animal life, and so on. But allegory, or, at least, precise allegory in which all meanings are fixed, is not, I think, what de la Mare was after. Speaking privately of T. S. Eliot, de la Mare declared: 'What I have against T. S. E. is that in *The Waste Land* he felt it necessary to give precise meanings and correspondences.'[7] To judge by his annotations to his books, de la Mare's reservations about *The Waste Land* in fact spread a little wider: he disliked how 'referential, self-centred and obscure' the poem was.[8] Still, it is telling that it is the 'precise meanings and correspondences' that de la Mare most objects to, not least because the nature of the objection indicates an unexpected similarity in reading habits between the two poets. Although the book of *The Listeners* didn't appear until 1912, Sir Henry Newbolt praises 'The Listeners' in a letter to Ella Coltman of November 1908, so it was presumably written earlier that year.[9] On 15 March 1908, the same year as T. S. Eliot purchased the book himself, de la Mare bought his copy of Arthur Symons's *The Symbolist Movement in Literature*. Though de la Mare may well have known the book already, it was a significant acquisition, for the de la Mare of *The Listeners* and *Peacock Pie* has a lot in common with the Symbolists. He shared their devotion to the work of Edgar Allan Poe (1809–49), whose 'The Raven' provides the obvious ancestor to the spectral knocking in 'The Listeners' and other 'knocking' poems by de la Mare. He was also, like the French Symbolists, exploring dreams and essences, and becoming less interested in the thing itself than in the effect

73

it happens to produce (see my commentary to 'The Bells'). One way of saying what is going on in 'The Listeners' and poems like it is that it is the work of a poet who, like Stéphane Mallarmé (1842–98) as described by Arthur Symons, seeks to 'evoke, by some elaborate, instantaneous magic of language, without the formality of an after all impossible description; to be, rather than to express'.[10]

In October 1908, de la Mare published one of his most suggestive tales, 'The Bird of Travel'. As Giles de la Mare[11] and, more recently, Angela Leighton, have pointed out, there are suggestive similarities between the short story and the poem.[12] In the tale, the boy narrator comes to a deserted house – a house to which he shall, much later, return. He finds a door on the latch: 'I tapped and listened; tapped and listened again; and, as if it were Echo herself, some hidden thrush's rapping of a snail's shell . . . was my only answer'.[13] When the Bird of Travel is then heard, it is 'as if some unearthly traveller were summoning from afar his strayed dog on the hillside!'[14] We hear too how two previous visitors have listened to the Bird of Travel and drunk in 'its forbidden song . . . And now, Hamilton lies far away, unburied amid the Andes, and Paul drowned in the Straits of Magellan.'[15]

Giles de la Mare also notes the resemblances between 'The Listeners' and 'The Story of This Book', the allegorical tale used to preface the anthology *Come Hither*. Comparison between it and 'The Listeners' lends credibility to the explanation for 'The Listeners' de la Mare gave Laurence Whistler in the 1950s: that it was 'about a man encountering a universe' (*a* man and *a* universe not 'man and the universe', lovers of exact correspondences should note).[16] Of Nahum Taroone, whose name is a rough anagram of Human Nature, Miss Taroone, whose relationship to Nahum is unclear, says:

> He has his two worlds. Take your time. Some day you
> too, I dare say, will go off on your travels. Remember
> that, like Nahum, you are as old as the hills which neither
> spend nor waste time, but dwell in it for ages, as if it were
> light or sunshine. Some day perhaps Nahum will shake
> himself free of Thrae [Earth] altogether. I don't *know*,
> myself, Simon. This house is enough for me, and what I
> remember of Sure Vine [Universe], compared with which
> Thrae is but the smallest of bubbles in a large glass.[17]

Later in the story, as the narrator comes to say goodbye and this time spend the night in Mr Taroone's room, he is informed that 'Mr Nahum may at this very moment be riding home. Have a candle alight.' That night he finds 'there were two minds in me as midnight drew on, almost two selves, the one busy with pen and ink, the other stealthily listening to every faintest sound [. . .] Steadily burned my candles; no sound of hoofs, no owl-cry, no knocking disturbed my peace.'[18]

Robert Frost, who hugely admired the poem, wrote that he 'once asked de la Mare if he had noticed anything queer about the verse in his own "The Listeners" and he answered that he hadnt [sic] noticed anything at all about the verse in it queer or unqueer'.[19] What had caught Frost's attention is the poem's curious double metre. Depending on how one performs them, it is possible to scan almost all its lines either with three stresses or with four. The difference isn't merely a matter of taste. Peter Howarth notes that if you don't stress that opening 'Is', the Traveller is giving us 'an honest question'; do so and you have a query that suspects the answer already.[20] Howarth goes on to note that the 'three-stress lines are also the ones that describe the positive *absence* of the listeners, felt in what doesn't happen' (the examples he gives are lines 9, 21 and 29).[21] On the other hand, the additional stresses in some lines are likewise appropriate – whether it be to the thronging on the dark stair, or the echoing through the shadowiness. However one *could* stress the poem, most reciters seem to begin by confidently giving the lines three stresses. It is only later – perhaps on line 3 and, more probably, line 7 – that a fourth stress tends to creep in. Because of this, Derek Attridge disregards the metrical ambiguity noticed by Frost and Howarth, claiming that the poem is based on a stress pattern of '3-3-4-3 quatrains', although Attridge does concede that 'as the poem proceeds the patterns of beats become less easy to perceive'.[22]

De la Mare's own recorded performance of the poem does roughly follow the 3-3-4-3 pattern suggested by Attridge.[23] Still, that's just one way of reciting it; de la Mare's own writings on metre are very alive to metrical ambiguity. For example, a note to *Come Hither* finds de la Mare demonstrating how Michael Drayton's 'Fair stood the wind for France' can be stressed in 'at least four ways'.[24] In that same note, de la Mare writes:

all poetry, unless its charm is to be wasted, should be *heard*, with the inward ear at least, if not with the outer; and the intonation, like the rhythm, is part and parcel of its meaning. Unless it be in accord with the thought and the feeling intended, it falsifies the poem. This is curiously true even of single words – that once were double. Stress lightly and raise the voice a little on the second or third syllable in each of the following words, and a meaning that may hitherto have been half-hidden slips up like a cuckoo out of a clock: gate*way*, lock*smith*, highway*man*, hard*bake*, draw*back*, skin*flint*, dream*land*, cup*board*, sea*worthy*, shoe*horn*.[25]

Sure enough, when de la Mare recites 'The Listeners', he stresses the second part of 'moonbeams' (l. 17) and 'moon-light' (l. 15), with very effective results. De la Mare concludes this note in *Come Hither* by pointing out how metrical discussion can 'add to one's knowledge, but not much to one's delight in the reading of poetry, and still less, I imagine, to the writing of it. In general, if you read a poem quietly over, first, to your head, then to your heart, most technical difficulties vanish like morning mist.'[26]

The Scarecrow

All winter through I bow my head
   Beneath the driving rain;
The North Wind powders me with snow
   And blows me black again;
At midnight in a maze of stars   5
   I flame with glittering rime,
And stand, above the stubble, stiff
   As mail at morning-prime.
But when that child, called Spring, and all
   His host of children, come,   10
Scattering their buds and dew upon
   These acres of my home,
Some rapture in my rags awakes;
   I lift void eyes and scan
The skies for crows, those ravening foes,   15
   Of my strange master, Man.
I watch him striding lank behind
   His clashing team, and know
Soon will the wheat swish body high
   Where once lay sterile snow;   20
Soon shall I gaze across a sea
   Of sun-begotten grain,
Which my unflinching watch hath sealed
   For harvest once again.

from *The Listeners and Other Poems* (1912)

A scarecrow is, of course, merely a couple of sticks dressed in some old clothes with maybe a hat on its head, made to look like a man in order to safeguard the crops. It is also one of those things of fascination for de la Mare, a decoy. Scarecrows are uncanny objects too, inanimate yet human-looking. They fit strangeness: the scarecrow in de la Mare's children's story of that name has been the haunt of fairies. In this poem, the scarecrow gets to speak. His tale is of what he knows from his life outside: the seasons in the fields, winter through to spring, summer through to harvest.

In the opening eight lines we move from rain to snow to frost. The 'maze of stars' (l. 5) is not so much the night sky as its reflection in the 'glittering rime' (l. 6), the frost upon the scarecrow. The scarecrow is presumably stiff as chain mail rather than the morning post, chain mail having the same qualities of glittering reflectiveness at dawn or 'morning-prime' (l. 8). Though 'The Scarecrow' is a poem which gives voice to the lifeless, there is a straightforward explanation to the change in him as the year goes on: the weather is altering his rags and giving him his purpose, protecting budding crops from the 'ravening' (l. 15) – hungry, but also raven-like – crows. In a world where personifications seem real gods and spirits, where Spring is a child leading his children, the sun is father to the grain: it is 'begotten' (l. 22) of him. When Man himself arrives upon the scene, there is a marriage of sound and image. We move from the 'clashing' team of plough horses, with an implied swish of the whip from the ploughman to the 'swish' of the 'body high' (l. 19) corn, whose waves convert the snow to 'sea' (l. 21).

De la Mare liked to reuse themes and titles, and in so doing revisit his earlier poems. *The Burning-Glass* (1945) contains another poem entitled 'The Scarecrow'. This one, which evidently captures the feelings of the dark days of the Second World War, allegorises its effigy much more explicitly. It is set in winter, and its scarecrow in an abandoned orchard is clearly an image of fallen man abandoned by his God. Even if the Symbolist style makes it much harder to interpret than the scarecrow in *The Burning-Glass*, the scarecrow in this poem seems an altogether more positive presence. Despite its having no definite indicators, the poem is open to being read as something like an allegory of Christ. Though not a man, or at least not in the usual sense, he appears to be one. Like Christ, the scarecrow is dead upon a cross, yet he rises again with the crops in the springtime. In the Bible and elsewhere, Christ is associated with parables of sowing and harvest, and the harvest is a traditional metaphor for the harvest of souls.

If 'The Scarecrow' is to be interpreted thus, that may not mean it is a wholly Christian poem. The scarecrow is both man-made and made in man's image and it is here presented as something more like a fertility god than the Christ of Christian doctrine. Moreover, it would be hard to maintain such an interpretation as definitive; there are other ways of reading the poem. For instance, the scarecrow could be an allegory of the poem itself, a lifeless thing made in man's image, which with its void eyes nonetheless looks over and responds to the world of humankind. That is one alternative, and I'm sure there are others.

Miss Loo

When thin-strewn memory I look through,
I see most clearly poor Miss Loo;
Her tabby cat, her cage of birds,
Her nose, her hair, her muffled words,
And how she'd open her green eyes, 5
As if in some immense surprise,
Whenever as we sat at tea
She made some small remark to me.
It's always drowsy summer when
From out the past she comes again; 10
The westering sunshine in a pool
Floats in her parlour still and cool;
While the slim bird its lean wires shakes,
As into piercing song it breaks;

Till Peter's pale-green eyes ajar 15
Dream, wake; wake, dream, in one brief bar.
And I am sitting, dull and shy,
And she with gaze of vacancy,
And large hands folded on the tray,
Musing the afternoon away; 20
Her satin bosom heaving slow
With sighs that softly ebb and flow,
And her plain face in such dismay,
It seems unkind to look her way:

Until all cheerful back will come   25
Her gentle gleaming spirit home:
And one would think that poor Miss Loo
Asked nothing else, if she had you.

from *The Listeners and Other Poems* (1912)

One might expect memory to be 'thick-strewn' rather than 'thin' (l. 1), given the way time amasses reminiscences. Thin-strewn memory is, however, easier to 'look through', and this is the case with the memory of Miss Loo.

Why is she 'poor' Miss Loo' (l. 2 and l. 27)? Is it because she is short of money? Or because the term is used in the habitual formulation of the adult world telling the boy how he must be company for 'poor Miss Loo' who never married, has had a difficult life and is all by herself – and at her age. Or is it because of something that troubles her when one sees 'her plain face in such dismay' (l. 23); is she 'poor' because of what will happen to her in her future and the narrator's past, something she foresees?

Miss Loo's 'green eyes' (l. 5) are disconcertingly close to the 'pale-green eyes ajar' (l. 15) (another unexpected yet perfect word choice) of the dreaming and waiting cat Peter, who seems the avatar of his mistress with her slow heaving satin bosom (for a curiously similar parallel between human and cat's eyes, see my note to 'Napoleon'). The 'dull and shy' (l. 17) boy trapped in her parlour is a little too like one of Miss Loo's slim, caged birds. Not only do the poem's last two lines imply that she does usually ask for quite a lot else besides, their wanting of 'you' may not be so much a humble ask as an all-enveloping demand.

Despite her being 'poor Miss Loo', the presentation of her isn't so very far from that of the eponymous dark presence in de la Mare's chilling story 'Seaton's Aunt', and yet she *is* 'poor Miss Loo'. She exists in a strange eternity of 'wester-ing' (l. 11), that is nearing the west and sunset – an age-old analogy for death. The 'slim bird' (l. 13) shaking the wires of the cage with its song is almost like her soul. The 'ebb and flow' (l. 22) of sighs seems also to be the ebb and flow of her life, her dismay as it leaves and her cheerfulness as her spirit returns home (ll. 25–6). We assume 'Peter' is the cat, but he might be the apostle, the key-holder of the gates of heaven, briefly waking then dreaming as if about to notice her and let her in. Her 'gaze of vacancy' (l. 18) looks like the look in the eyes of the departed.

In a poem that enacts a curious suspension of time, the very language is curiously suspended. One might expect that 'The westering sunshine in a pool' (l. 11) would refer simply to a pool of light, yet it floats 'still and cool' as if it were floating in a pond of air. Miss Loo exists in her own little eternity: 'It's always drowsy summer when/ From out the past she comes again' (ll. 9–10). Furthermore, there is a parallel between her ebb and flow between life and death and her disappearance from and return to memory.

De la Mare's iambic tetrameter couplets are a whole world away from, say, their witty employment by Andrew Marvell; instead, their effect is lingering and hypnotic. The rhymes act as if they might also be part of a larger structure that echoes, ponders and recalls rather than quickly moving on. The rhyme at the poem's end reprises that of its opening. The rhyme of lines 19–20 quickly returns in lines 23–4, in the lingered moment of watching the rising and falling satin bosom of Miss Loo 'musing the afternoon away'.

Winter Dusk

Dark frost was in the air without,
   The dusk was still with cold and gloom,
When less than even a shadow came
   And stood within the room.

But of the three around the fire,   5
   None turned a questioning head to look,
Still read a clear voice, on and on,
   Still stooped they o'er their book.

The children watched their mother's eyes
   Moving on softly line to line;   10
It seemed to listen too – that shade,
   Yet made no outward sign.

The fire-flames crooned a tiny song,
   No cold wind stirred the wintry tree;
The children both in Faërie dreamed   15
   Beside their mother's knee.

And nearer yet that spirit drew
   Above that heedless one, intent
Only on what the simple words
   Of her small story meant.   20

No voiceless sorrow grieved her mind,
　　No memory her bosom stirred,
Nor dreamed she, as she read to two,
　　'Twas surely three who heard.

Yet when, the story done, she smiled   25
　　From face to face, serene and clear,
A love, half dread, sprang up, as she
　　Leaned close and drew them near.

from *The Listeners and Other Poems* (1912)

'Winter Dusk' is a mystery. We are given a number, but not all, of the pieces with which to solve it, and there are dark corners to be completed only by our guesses. Who is it who has cast the 'less than even a shadow' (l. 3) that stands inside the room? The absent husband and father? Surely he would have been more interested in seeing his wife and children again rather than in listening to the words of the story? More likely it is the spirit of a dead child, presumably the sibling of those who listen around the fire, who has come in from the cold to join them.

But how does this spirit listen, and to what? There is another sound beside the small story, a 'tiny song' (l. 13) crooned by the fire like a mother singing to an infant. For the child, maternal comfort and singing gives way to watching a mother's eyes reading and, before long, to reading for oneself; tiny songs give way to 'small' stories, sitting on mother's knee gives way to standing 'beside' (l. 16) it. But only when an infant does not die. Such little sights and sounds and distances – the crooning fire, the children suddenly far away from the mother and in the land of 'Faërie' – may themselves summon a dead child to the back of the mother's mind and an expectation of a third child not seen as she surveys her children. No wonder she feels the need to pull the two children she has in close.

Each stanza of 'Winter Dusk' contains three lines of iambic tetrameter followed by a line of iambic trimeter, the way each stanza draws in at its close being ideally suited to the drawing in of the action in a number of them. The carefully measured metrical regularity is likewise a close fit for its domestic subject; it also allows one's listening mind to register the slightest deviation from the usual rhythm, if only at an unconscious level. So when the line 'When less than even a shadow came' (l. 3) has an extra unstressed syllable – not enough of a change for one to notice it has happened, but just enough to register some tiny extra presence – it is the poem's metre as well as its meaning letting in less than a shadow.

The Keys of Morning

While at her bedroom window once,
 Learning her task for school,
Little Louisa lonely sat
 In the morning clear and cool,
She slanted her small bead-brown eyes   5
 Across the empty street,
And saw Death softly watching her
 In the sunshine pale and sweet.

His was a long lean sallow face;
 He sat with half-shut eyes,   10
Like an old sailor in a ship
 Becalmed 'neath tropic skies.
Beside him in the dust he had set
 His staff and shady hat;
These, peeping small, Louisa saw   15
 Quite clearly where she sat –
The thinness of his coal-black locks,
 His hands so long and lean
They scarcely seemed to grasp at all
 The keys that hung between: 20
Both were of gold, but one was small,
 And with this last did he
Wag in the air, as if to say,
 'Come hither, child, to me!'

Louisa laid her lesson book   25
    On the cold window-sill;
And in the sleepy sunshine house
    Went softly down, until
She stood in the half-opened door,
    And peeped. But strange to say,   30
Where Death just now had sunning sat
    Only a shadow lay:
Just the tall chimney's round-topped cowl,
    And the small sun behind,
Had with its shadow in the dust   35
    Called sleepy Death to mind.
But most she thought how strange it was
    Two keys that he should bear,
And that, when beckoning, he should wag
    The littlest in the air.   40

from *The Listeners and Other Poems* (1912)

The resonant title has its chief explanation in the keys and time of day we find in the poem. It can also be construed metaphorically. Louisa is in the morning of her life; nightfall is for sleeping. This morning, however, little Louisa has let herself drift off in the 'sleepy sunshine house' (l. 27), when she should be doing her homework.

The way Louisa sits, slanting her 'bead-brown eyes' (l. 5) is shadowed by the way Death sits with 'half-shut eyes' (l. 10) but also by how Louisa later peeps through 'the half-opened door' (l. 29). A pattern is formed of half-seeing and half-opening – Death and Louisa half-see each other, are half-awake or half-asleep – which makes us recognise, if in our own somewhat dreamy way, that death's door, like that of Louisa's house and eyes, now stands ajar. The poem which precedes 'The Keys of Morning' and which is its companion poem in *The Listeners*, is 'The Sleeper'. In it, Ann enters a 'house of sleep' and sees her mother asleep upon a chair, her face trans-formed. The transformation is clearly a premonition of her mother's death. Ann tiptoes out again, but while Ann sees her premonition of death and is afraid, Little Louisa is 'lonely' (l. 3) and when beckoned to by death, half-follows it outside. She has been beguiled.

The question that so puzzles Louisa at the end, why Death should have two keys, and 'wag/ The littlest in the air' (l. 39–40), likewise foxed the philosopher and critic Owen Barfield. De la Mare answered his question about it by saying 'one was for Death's big door, the other for the little'.[1] In addition to having a big door for the grown-ups, Death has a door the right size for little Louisa.

At the close of the poem, Louisa *almost* believes that the decoy that has brought her to her door is no more than the shadow of the chimney pot. Yet the apparition of death becalmed upon his journey has been astonishingly vivid, and more so than a straightforward optical illusion would be. Louisa's half-sleep has put her in a hypnagogic state. In *Behold, This Dreamer!*, de la Mare collects a number of explanations and eyewitness accounts of these states, including his own, and writes:

> In a brief time, waking consciousness may be for an
> instant [. . .] repeatedly submerged, and may repeatedly
> retrieve isolated peephole glimpses of an imagery at least
> as vivid as anything bestowed by fancy on the eye of
> day – glimpses, too, which occasionally have an aptness
> and a hint of profound significance usually denied to or
> unnoticed in the actual of the waking day.[2]

Little Louisa's hypnagogic state has taught her a truth unlikely to be featured in her homework.

Forrest Reid (1875–1947), the novelist and friend of Walter de la Mare, observes in his study of de la Mare's work that '"The sunshine pale and sweet" has literally the effect of an incantation' and that 'the Pre-Raphaelite detail makes the whole thing concrete and authentic.'[3] The incantatory effect here that is most easy to pin down is a general one: the way de la Mare employs and adapts a balladic metre. If 'The sunshine pale and sweet' seems particularly incantatory, it is because of the way de la Mare deploys the metre to impart a particular fullness to its syllables. The pair of stresses one naturally gives 'sunshine' slows down the line, a slowing process that has already been started by similar effects in the other lines in the second half of the stanza. This slowing down of the lines then carries on to stretch out the open vowel sounds of 'pale' and 'sweet', making sure that they are accorded a longer quantity. We too have been beguiled.

The Pigs and the Charcoal-Burner

The old Pig said to the little pigs,
  'In the forest is truffles and mast,
Follow me then, all ye little pigs,
   Follow me fast!'

The Charcoal-burner sat in the shade   5
  His chin on his thumb,
And saw the big Pig and the little pigs,
   Chuffling come.

He watched 'neath a green and giant bough,
  And the pigs in the ground   10
Made a wonderful grizzling and gruzzling
   And greedy sound.

And when, full-fed, they were gone, and Night
  Walked her starry ways,
He stared with his cheeks in his hands   15
   At his sullen blaze.

from *Peacock Pie: A Book of Rhymes* (1913)

Charcoal-burning was a lengthy process. A mound or kiln was built. Once lit, this would require tending for several days and nights to ensure that the air-starved fire, and with it the desired slow carbonisation of the wood, was properly in hand. Since mounds and kilns were often constructed in forests and away from human habitation, the job tended to be a solitary one. Hungry too. De la Mare's short story, 'The Game at Cards', begins with a charcoal-burner who has very little food, sitting beside his burning mound eating a supper of 'black bread and onions', while the red fire is 'slowly gnawing its way inch by inch through the logs of fragrant wood'.[1]

For pig and piglet on the other hand, the forest can be a place of plenty. It was where they were taken to graze, its being full of 'mast' (l. 2), that is the fruits of the forest: acorns, beechnuts and other softer growths ('mast' is a word which in origin meant literally 'food for swine'). The practice of keeping pigs in woodlands to consume mast is referred to as 'acorning' or 'pannage'.[2] Pigs have a fine sense of smell and, probably because of a similarity between the scent of the truffle and the pheromones of the boar pig, an especially fine nose for truffles. Whether it be the Traveller's horse in 'The Listeners' or these greedy pigs, de la Mare is alive to animal existence and the straightforward delight in eating that seems to go with it. The 'grizzling and guzzling/ And greedy sound' (ll. 11–12) of the feeding pigs feels particularly relished. 'Chuffling' (l. 8) is a low snuffling.

Henry Charles Duffin interprets the pigs as the charcoal-burner's dream.[3] They are certainly an object of the charcoal-burner's contemplation. As opposed to being in a sociable a happy, guzzling family, the charcoal-burner is left to a 'sullen blaze' (l. 16): the word 'sullen' comes from 'sol', the Anglo-Norman French for 'solitary'. There is no more immediate satisfaction than that of some pigs having a good scoff; there are few occupations which required more solitary patience than charcoal-burning. Both transform the forest: one makes mast, food for energy and instant gratification, while the other takes the 'green and giant bough' (l. 9) and turns it to carbon, a substance which itself may be used to burn at high temperatures. It is not the wood itself, it is its after-image, the wood transformed, that interests the solitary charcoal-burner.

The pigs themselves may be transformed by the charcoal-burner's quiet, solitary reflection. The pigs arrive 'fast' – here, closely or tightly as well as quickly – at the end of the poem 'Night' walks (ll. 13–14) and the benighted charcoal-burner is left unmoving, staring at his fire. Whose existence is preferable, that of the charcoal-burner or that of the pigs?

All That's Past

Very old are the woods;
   And the buds that break
Out of the brier's boughs,
   When March winds wake,
So old with their beauty are –   5
   Oh, no man knows
Through what wild centuries
   Roves back the rose.

Very old are the brooks;
   And the rills that rise   10
Where snow sleeps cold beneath
   The azure skies
Sing such a history
   Of come and gone,
Their every drop is as wise   15
   As Solomon.

Very old are we men;
   Our dreams are tales
Told in dim Eden
   By Eve's nightingales;   20
We wake and whisper awhile,
   But, the day gone by,

Silence and sleep like fields
  Of amaranth lie.

from *The Listeners and Other Poems* (1912)

The Cambridge critic F. R. Leavis (1895–1978) writes in *New Bearings in English Poetry* (1932): 'Perhaps only a reader familiar with Mr de la Mare would note that in this first stanza he is playing in particular on reminiscences of Sleeping Beauty. The suggestion may seem unnecessary, but it is not random, and it serves to point the observation that in general, however serious his intention, he is exploiting the fairy-tale stratum of experience.'[1] There's no doubt de la Mare valued Sleeping Beauty (Leavis is probably thinking of the Sleeping Beauty chapter in de la Mare's 1904 novel *Henry Brocken*) and indeed the fairy tale in general, but, beyond some vague echo through the mention of centuries and brier roses, there is no evidence de la Mare is playing on such reminiscences here. Moreover, Leavis's belief that this is comforting escapism rests on a failure to read the poem properly: the state of briers and roses in the first stanza is in clear contradistinction to the state of humans as delineated in the last stanza, a state which may not be comforting at all.

'All That's Past' is a poem about time, and in particular the contrast between the cyclical time of the natural world and the linear time and eternity familiar from the Christian religion. In its first stanza, that time is the renewable time of plants. Woods and the 'brier's boughs' (l. 3) wake in spring-time, as they have done for years beyond man's counting. The rose bush itself has roved back over wild centuries, briers being uncultivated roses free to move by re-rooting as well as by the seeding of their hips. In the second stanza the emphasis is again upon transience and renewal. Snow may sleep, but 'rills' (l. 10) (small streams) rise as snow melts. Since snow is melting, again it may be springtime. If skies are clear and azure over snow, that will pass, 'every drop' (l. 15) of those rills reminding the observer how the snow which melts to water will one day transpire, rising into the air again, before it clouds and falls once more. In that way, their every drop is as wise as was the wisest king in the Bible.

The last stanza of 'All That's Past' turns to 'we men' (l. 17). 'We' too are very old. But while in that sense no different from the rose, 'we' dream stories of the nightingales of Eden. Our dreams are, then, tales of songs of nature heard before our fall from innocence, those songs having presumably been at one with the natural process of death and rebirth found in the first two stanzas. And yet, however we dream of Eden, we are exiled from its bounds; we wake (l. 21), and, unable to sing like nightingales, 'whisper awhile' (l. 21) before silence and sleep 'like fields/ Of amaranth lie' (ll. 23–24). The mention of amaranth is an allusion to Aesop's fable in which the amaranth envies the rose its beauty and perfume and the rose envies the perennial amaranth its immortality, an association that is played on by Milton in Book III of *Paradise Lost* (ll. 352–64). In de la Mare's poem, the rose is mortal: it lives, dies and carries on as part of the same process of existence as snow, brooks, clouds and rainfall and even nightingales. And 'we men' (l. 17)? Our 'day gone by' (l. 22), 'we' face the 'Silence and sleep' (l. 23) that is death. We have in our minds and wishes the prospect of fields of amaranth, the Elysian Fields of the eternal afterlife. Can this console us for our exile from the world of nature? It depends on how we read the last word of the poem. Those 'fields of amaranth' may, after all, be no more than a 'lie' (l. 24).

Like '"The Hawthorn Hath a Deathly Smell"', 'All That's Past' pushes de la Mare's interest in the music of consonance, assonance and alliteration and the musical potential of various rhetorical devices, including inversions, to its fullest extent. Its prosody is at once carefully patterned and flexible, and contains metrical ambiguities (do we, for instance, stress the 'Ve' of 'Very' or glide into each stanza's first line with an unstressed syllable)? Each stanza begins with, and the first and last stanza close with, an inversion of subject and object, an anastrophe. This has an effect on the sense as well as the sound of the poem. Writing 'Roves back the rose' (l. 8) is not the same thing as writing 'The rose roves back': the inversion stresses the verb, imbuing 'Roves' with a sense of dynamic movement, thus making clear that this isn't a lightly used metaphor but a description of the actual progress of the plant.

In his memoir *Goodbye to All That*, Robert Graves recalls telling de la Mare:

what hours of worry he must have had over the lines:

> Ah [sic], no man knows
> Through what wild centuries
>   Roves back the rose.

and how, in the end, he had been dissatisfied.

According to Graves, de la Mare ruefully admitted that he was forced to leave the assonance of roves and rose because no synonym for 'roves' seemed strong enough.[2] The story of the encounter has been skewed by Graves's love of point-scoring: Paul Edwards observes that Graves must have known very well that de la Mare chose the word precisely because of the assonance and not despite it; the purpose of the anecdote is Graves's 'childish need to demonstrate his own superior poetic taste'.[3] The music of the poem does indeed need the assonance: the 'o' sounds in 'Roves back the rose' answer those in 'Oh, no man knows' (l. 6). 'Roves' also allows de la Mare to keep up the pattern of alliteration set up in the earlier lines and have 'r's and 'b' that pick up on but reverse 'buds that break' (l. 2) and 'brier's boughs' (l. 3). It was the meaning not the sound – or rather the need to have the right meaning *and* the right sound – which gave de la Mare trouble. Ella Coltman had objected to the original choice of 'Roams'.[4] De la Mare at first defended the word on the ground that 'roams meant the wild rose shoots tangling back across time to the primal hip!'[5] But, bowing to Coltman's objection, de la Mare then tried 'roots' and 'climbs' (the latter of which would make an assonance with 'wild'), before finally hitting upon 'roves'.[6]

'The Hawthorn Hath a Deathly Smell'

The flowers of the field
   Have a sweet smell;
Meadowsweet, tansy, thyme,
   And faint-heart pimpernel;
But sweeter even than these,   5
   The silver of the may
Wreathed is with incense for
   The Judgment Day.

An apple, a child, dust,
   When falls the evening rain,   10
Wild briar's spicèd leaves,
   Breathe memories again;
With further memory fraught,
   The silver of the may
Wreathed is with incense for   15
   The Judgment Day.

Eyes of all loveliness –
   Shadow of strange delight,
Even as a flower fades
   Must thou from sight;   20
But oh, o'er thy grave's mound,
   Till come the Judgment Day,

Wreathed shall with incense be
Thy sharp-thorned may.

from *The Listeners and Other Poems* (1912)

Hawthorn blossom, the 'may', contains trimethylamine, an ingredient of putrefaction. The stench is much more noticeable in the once more numerous Midland variety than it is in the more fragrant, common hawthorn.[1] While the quotation marks around the title presumably denote a piece of proverbial folk wisdom, I suspect the precise formulation of the saying is down to the way the archaic 'hath' adds to the pattern of 'th' sounds (that 'th' is the digraph which replaces the Middle English letter 'thorn' is also worth noting, though probably a coincidence). The archaism also calls to mind poetry of the sixteenth and seventeenth centuries, including 'The Day of Judgement' by Henry Vaughan (1621–95) in which from 'each forgotten grave . . . the dead, like flowers arise'. [2]

While meadowsweet (l. 3), the Queen of the Meadow, has romantic connotations, according to the Worcestershire folk belief its sweet scent can cause a sleep from which one might not recover.[3] Tansy (l. 3) was used to preserve dead bodies from corruption. In Somerset at least, thyme, like may, was thought dangerous to keep indoors because it smelt of death.[4] By 'pimpernel' (l. 4), I presume de la Mare means what he says – a little red flower betokening a faint heart (the red or scarlet pimpernel is the male of the species).

'Wreathed' (l. 7) is in accord with the word's root sense of 'wound round' but naturally also evokes floral wreathes, particularly those at funerals. Religious services are 'wreathed' with incense: in a high Anglican service, this would be white, scented smoke from silver censers: the image may draw on de la Mare's days as a chorister in St Paul's Cathedral. 'Judgment Day' (l. 8) is the day when the dead will be reunited with their bodies, the moment when putrefaction stops. The Bible figures that judgement of the saved and the damned in terms of a tree:

> Ye shall know them by their fruits. Do men gather grapes of thorns, or figs of thistles? Even so every good tree bringeth forth good fruit; but a corrupt tree bringeth forth evil fruit. A good tree cannot bring forth evil fruit, neither *can* a corrupt tree bring forth good fruit. Every tree that bringeth not forth good fruit is hewn down, and cast into the fire. Wherefore by their fruits ye shall know them. (Matthew 7, 16–20)

There is also an English tradition that the crown of thorns worn by Jesus on the cross was made of hawthorn.

'An apple, a child, dust,' (l. 9) in evening rain, though in itself evocative, may also recall the apple eaten by Eve and Adam in the Garden of Eden and the curse which followed it: 'Thorns also and thistles shall [the ground] bring forth to thee; and thou shalt eat the herb of the field; in the sweat of thy face shalt thou eat bread, till thou return unto the ground; for out of it wast thou taken: for dust thou *art*, and unto dust shalt thou return.' (Genesis 3, 18–19) As elsewhere in de la Mare, the word 'child' implies the lost Eden of childhood. Memories of Eden give way to reminders of mortality, and possible immortality: in remembering the Fall, we remember the death to come.

'Eyes of all loveliness' (l. 17) recalls 'the White-thorn, lovely May,/ Opens her many lovely eyes' of William Blake's poem

Milton.[5] The comparison between 'Eyes of all loveliness' (l. 17) and eye-like flowers fading seems to bring in another person and another perspective: an individual 'thou' with lovely eyes. When this 'thou' dies, a sharp-thorned may shall linger on. The sentiment is reminiscent of the Elizabethan sonneteers promising the loved one immortality in rhyme, as when Shakespeare in Sonnet 18 declares: 'So long as men can breathe or eyes can see,/ So long lives this, and this gives life to thee.'

The hawthorn doesn't just smell of death; its smell is also reckoned to be redolent of sex. It is associated with May fertility rites and in medieval literature with human romantic and sexual love. There are also traditions which make the hawthorn a dwelling place for the fairies.[6]

Theresa Whistler points out that '"The Hawthorn Hath a Deathly Smell"' functions as a covert love poem to Naomi Royde-Smith (1875–1964). Royde Smith worked at the *Westminster Gazette*, becoming literary editor of the *Saturday Westminster Gazette* in 1912. At the time when de la Mare encountered her in person, in February 1911, she wrote verse, and in future years, she would become a prolific novelist and biographer. De la Mare fell deeply under her spell. '"The Hawthorn Hath a Deathly Smell"', was written shortly after the two had met before going on to share an apple at Royde-Smith's house. 'The Sweetbriar somehow is you', wrote de la Mare to Royde-Smith on 8 April 1911, in 'its medley of things I can't understand.'[7]

A Song of Enchantment

A Song of Enchantment I sang me there,
In a green – green wood, by waters fair,
Just as the words came up to me
I sang it under the wild wood tree.

Widdershins turned I, singing it low, 5
Watching the wild birds come and go;
No cloud in the deep dark blue to be seen
Under the thick-thatched branches green.

Twilight came; silence came;
The planet of evening's silver flame; 10
By darkening paths I wandered through
Thickets trembling with drops of dew.

But the music is lost and the words are gone
Of the song I sang as I sat alone,
Ages and ages have fallen on me – 15
On the wood and the pool and the elder tree.

from *Peacock Pie: A Book of Rhymes* (1913)

'Enchantment' derives from '*chanter*', the French for 'to sing' from the Latin '*cantare*'. At its root then, an enchantment is a magic effected by singing or chanting into something or someone. The narrator of the poem is, knowingly or not, performing a spell. To turn 'Widdershins' is to turn counter-clockwise and to move in the direction opposite to that taken by the sun, a potent form of spell-making. In the traditional tale of Childe Rowland, for instance, Burd Ellen accidentally goes Widdershins around a church and as a consequence is imprisoned in the dark tower of the King of Elfland. De la Mare evidently had the superstition in mind when he made Arthur Lawford, the hero of his 1910 novel *The Return*, become possessed by the spirit of the libertine Nicholas Sabathier in the old churchyard in Widderstone, a place name that sounds far too close to the direction to be a coincidence.

The elder tree (l. 16) is associated with witchcraft and the goddess figure of the Elder Mother, whose traces turn up in English and Northern European superstition. She is also present in the pages of Hans Christian Andersen's story 'The Elder Tree Mother', where she is conjured up by a cup of elder tea. Under its influence, and under her spell, many years seem to have passed, though in fact scarcely any time has elapsed. Chris Howkins, in his book *The Elder: The Mother Tree of Folklore* notes that in 1776 the prominent doctor William Withering declared 'The whole plant hath a narcotic smell; it is not well to sleep under its shade.'[1] Traditional herbals such as the edition of Nicholas Culpeper's *Complete Herbal* in de la Mare's personal library state that the elder tree is a plant under the sign of Venus, the evening planet.

Along with the supernatural ones, there are natural explanations for the powers of this song of enchantment. Low singing or chanting can induce a trance-like state. Consequently, a child singing to itself may well feel this sense of lost time. The poem has that sense, familiar from other de la Mare poems of childhood, of a past child self being at one with the wild, natural world. During the moment of enchantment, the narrator is singing with that unpremeditated art Keats and Shelley envied in the nightingale and skylark. That moment gives way to loss and the disenchantment of the present. Poems, particularly those in lyric metres such as this, may have similar properties and indeed, as de la Mare knew, have been termed 'enchantments'.[2]

Manuscript evidence suggests that this poem was not written before 1911, the year de la Mare met Royde-Smith. De la Mare was still adding to *Peacock Pie* (1913) after *The Listeners* (1912) had gone to press, and some of his feelings for Royde-Smith become hidden in rhymes whose ostensive topics seem suitable for children. An obvious case is 'Bewitched', whose speaker has been called by a 'lady of witchcraft' and who has now become, as de la Mare must have for a while become himself, 'A stranger to my kin'. If 'A Song of Enchantment' also encodes the enchantments of Royde-Smith, the trick of transformation has been performed so thoroughly that it is impossible to be sure. Still, the presence of Venus, the goddess of love and those sensual 'Thickets trembling with drops of dew' (l. 12) give some credence to such speculation.

The Bees' Song

Thousandz of thornz there be
On the Rozez where gozez
The Zebra of Zee:
Sleek, striped, and hairy,
The steed of the Fairy   5
Princess of Zee.

Heavy with blossomz be
The Rozez that growzez
In the thickets of Zee.
Where grazez the Zebra,   10
Marked *Abracadeeebra*,
Of the Princess of Zee.

And he nozez the poziez
Of the Rozez that growzez
So luvez'm and free,   15
With an eye, dark and wary,
In search of a Fairy,
Whose Rozez he knowzez
Were not honeyed for he,
But to breathe a sweet incense   20
To solace the Princess
Of far-away Zzzee.

from *Peacock Pie: A Book of Rhymes* (1913)

'The Bees' Song' is, first of all, what it sounds like: buzzing zees from buzzing bees that conjure a whimsical, light and summery world. A poem to appeal to children, even very young ones, it sings of a zebra and a fairy princess. As such, it is a charming successor to Anon's:

> If Moses supposes his toeses are roses,
> Then Moses supposes erroneously;
> For nobody's toeses are posies or roses,
> As Moses supposes his toeses to be.

But it is a richer successor. Not just the ears but all the senses bring us the world of the bees: there is the look of the stripy zebra going amidst the roses and the stripy bees; there is the touch of the rose on the zebra's nose and the anticipated scratch of the thorns; there are the scents of the flowers and the incense-like honey.

For grown-ups, there is quite a good literary joke. One can find a similar number of zeds, or rather 'zees', standing in for esses in the Dorset dialect poems of William Barnes (1801–86); de la Mare may have particularly had in mind his poem 'Bees A-Zwarmen'. These Dorset bees may also sound a little American: de la Mare employs the standard American version of the alphabet's last letter and the American pronunciation of 'zebra'. De la Mare had still to visit the States, and there were as yet no 'talkies' to make American accents and usage familiar to the ears of an English reader, so it is fairly safe to say that he regarded zebra and zee as acceptable English variations rather than as principally American.

That said, de la Mare did use *Webster's American Dictionary of the English Language*, and it was to this that he referred when defending himself to a nine-year-old schoolboy who had complained of his use of 'shoon' for shoes in another *Peacock Pie* rhyme, 'Silver'.[1]

If 'The Bees' Song' is a sweet poem, it is one that barely conceals a threat. This zebra is getting on fine for the moment: as long as the bees aren't too fussed about height and colour, they might overlook his sex, size and species and mistake him for a nectar-gathering sister. But this isn't safe grazing for an interloper: there are thousands of thorns here and this zebra knows well that these flowers are not for him, but to be honeyed in order to make a sweet incense that can travel to the far away Princess, his mistress. And though the fact is never mentioned in the poem, bees also have stings.

One suspects that de la Mare has more on his mind than apiculture. The poem must have something to do with words and letters. '*Abracadeeebra*' (l. 11) is, more or less, the magical sound of the first five letters of the alphabet, and zee is, of course, the last. If he is black and white and marked '*Abracadeeebra*' in the coloured world of the bees, this zebra does not just look like an outsized monochromatic bee but also like a printed page. Bees make songs to buzz in the moment. They also make honey. They take nectar and change it into something sweet and incensed that can be stored and transported – here to the Princess of Zee. Zebras have no such skill, but a zebra marked '*Abracadeeebra*' might magically imitate a bee, in black and white if not in full colour.

The Princess of Zee is a far away and sleepy sort of

princess. As the end of the poem catches a few zeds, the land of Zee becomes a kingdom of sleep. Perhaps the only way to get to her is in dreams. And when one stops to think about it, the manufacture of honey is rather like dreaming: the stuff of days gets gathered in from all sorts of places to be mixed and changed into a different and new substance, yet one which retains some savour of its origins. For similar reasons, making honey is also something like the writing of poems. Indeed, since honey is also a preserve and poems can, to an extent, preserve what they describe, it seems the parallel between honey and poems is even better than it is with dreams.

Naomi Royde-Smith's biographer, Jill Benton, and de la Mare's biographer, Theresa Whistler, don't agree about the rights and wrongs of the relationship between the two: Whistler's Royde-Smith is something of a self-involved temptress; Benton's de la Mare is somewhat selfish and, initially at least, keener on a physical relationship. But the biographers do concur that this was more an affair of the head and the heart than one of the body: de la Mare didn't want to leave his wife and family, and was less focused on pleasures of the flesh than on encountering Royde-Smith as a ghost and a dream; Royde-Smith, who was coming out of a lesbian relationship, seems to have enjoyed being de la Mare's muse, and his being something of a male muse to her, more than she was attracted to the idea of being his mistress. If Royde-Smith was a ghost for de la Mare, to her he was a bee. Benton notices how in her memoir of de la Mare and in the thinly veiled portraits of him in her fiction, Royde-Smith repeatedly use bees' honey-making as a metaphor for the strange transformation of life into art and attributes this notion to him.[2]

Aspects of 'The Bees' Song' were no doubt meant to be fully intelligible to no one beyond Royde-Smith and de la Mare; nevertheless, I am fairly confident that the Princess of Zee is an outfit for Royde-Smith and that de la Mare is playing the front and back halves underneath the costume of that zebra. I would also note that that Zebra of Zee looks and sounds a little like the *Westminster Gazette*, for which de la Mare was a regular contributor. The honey of the bees is presumably the poetry de la Mare is writing and sending, which will not show the flowers of his love but its trans-formed state.

Those thorns must be the perils attendant on grazing among the flowers. This is a poem that is happy with sweet nosings and worried about pricks. The letter zed or zee comes from the Phoenician '*zayin*', which means sword. That in modern Hebrew slang the word is also used to mean 'penis' can't have been known by de la Mare, but he might have guessed it.[3]

The Honey Robbers

There were two Fairies, Gimmul and Mel,
Loved Earth Man's honey passing well;
Oft at the hives of his tame bees
They would their sugary thirst appease.

When even began to darken to night,   5
They would hie along in the fading light,
With elf-locked hair and scarlet lips,
And small stone knives to slit the skeps,
So softly not a bee inside
Should hear the woven straw divide.   10
And then with sly and greedy thumbs
Would rifle the sweet honeycombs.
And drowsily drone to drone would say,
'A cold, cold wind blows in this way';
And the great Queen would turn her head   15
From face to face, astonishèd,
And, though her maids with comb and brush
Would comb and soothe and whisper, 'Hush!'
About the hive would shrilly go
A keening – keening, to and fro;   20
At which those robbers 'neath the trees
Would taunt and mock the honey-bees,
And through their sticky teeth would buzz
Just as an angry hornet does.

And when this Gimmul and this Mel   25
Had munched and sucked and swilled their fill,
Or ever Man's first cock should crow
Back to their Faërie Mounds they'd go.
Edging across the twilight air,
Thieves of a guise remotely fair.   30

from *Peacock Pie: A Book of Rhymes* (1913)

Gimmul and Mel are old-time fairies. Not only do they 'hie' (l. 6), rather than 'go quickly', they raid 'skeps' (l. 8), bee hives made of woven straw that fell from favour among bee-keepers in the nineteenth century. The two have proper fairy hairstyles too: they are 'elf-locked' (l. 7), the traditional reason for children finding their hair tangled: elf-locks turn up in Mercutio's speech in Act I, Sc. 4 of *Romeo and Juliet* where Queen Mab, Queen of the Fairies, 'plaits the manes of horses in the night,/ And bakes the elflocks in foul sluttish hairs,/ Which once untangled, much misfortune bodes.' Similarly traditional are the fairies' cutting instruments: their knives are stone and not metal because fairies may not touch iron. Their homes are 'Faërie Mounds', the ancient tumuli or earthworks in which fairies were said to reside – what the Irish call *sídhe*, the realms of the dead and of the Other World.

Mel is the Latin for 'honey', but Gimmul is more mysterious. *Gimel* is the third letter of the Semitic alphabet, which gave rise to 'c' and 'g'.[1] Written on a *dreidel*, the four-sided spinning top traditionally used on the Jewish holiday of Hanukkah, it means *gantz* (everything); the player whose dreidel lands on the gimel gets to keep all the goodies, which may well include honey.[2] 'Gimmal' is also an English word current in Shakespeare's time that denotes a finger ring made so that it could be divided into two or three separate rings; it could also be a term for joints, links and connecting parts. I'm not certain whether Gimmul's name signifies either one of these or something else, but the former explanation fits the poem well.

Metaphors about poets and honey stretch back a long way.

The Greek lyric poet Pindar (*c.* 518–438 BC) fell asleep and, so the story goes, bees plastered his lips with honey, thus beginning his sweet-voiced poetic career. In Plato's *Ion*, Socrates, no great fan of poets, declares that inspired poets are like the bees winging their way from flower to flower and turning them to honey. Yet bee metaphors only fly so far. De la Mare may have liked the idea of poetry being like honey in the way it transformed what was gathered from many a flower. However, when he stopped to think about it, the life of a bee must have had considerably less appeal. Honey-making bees are female; male bees are drones, stingless creatures who eat the honey yet do not toil to make it and who are slaughtered by the workers when their potential for reproductive usefulness has passed. Drones have therefore become synonymous with unproductive idleness among males (in the P. G. Wodehouse stories, the work-shy Bertie Wooster's club is called The Drones). Poets male and female may like to think they are industrious and socially useful, but society is likely to disagree. And how many poets really want to identify with a creature that is entirely chaste, has no individuality, no freedom from the state and which toils itself to death in a matter of weeks? Thought about like that, who wouldn't prefer to be a robber fairy – or even a moth?

Maurice Maeterlinck's (1862–1949) writings as a Symbolist playwright and poet make an interesting comparison to the poetry of de la Mare and seem to have been an influence on them. Here, though, it isn't the Belgian author's imaginative work but his study *The Life of the Bee* (which de la Mare refers to in *Come Hither*) that informs the writing. Maeterlinck describes how:

the great honey thief, the huge sphinx atropos, the sinister
butterfly that bears a death's head on its back, penetrates
into the hive, humming its own strange note, which acts
as a kind of irresistible incantation; the news spreads
quickly from group to group, and from the guards at the
threshold to the workers on the furthest combs, the whole
population quivers.[3]

It's a potent analogy for the incantatory poet. In 'The Honey
Robbers' the behaviour of the moth has been taken on by
fairies. As stand-ins for poets, we have, rather than those
slaving bees, this wonderfully naughty, thieving, imitative
and sweet-toothed pair stealing honey from a well-ordered
civilisation to feed the Other World, the Land of Faerie
that is also the Land of the Dead. Poetry too, that place of
shadows, enchantments and of ghosts, may belong there.
In 'The Story of This Book' in de la Mare's *Come Hither*,
'THEOTHERWORLDE' is the title that the absent Nahum
Taroone has given to his anthology.

While younger readers will identify with the fairies' love of
the sweet stuff, the soft dividing of the woven straw in order
to rifle for honey combs and the way they munch, suck and
swill 'their fill' (l. 26) before cockcrow may well bring to adult
minds the pleasures of the bedroom. Not only is 'The Honey
Robbers' a sexy poem, it's a sexually confusing one too: which
sex *are* Gimmul and Mel? Are the honey robbers avatars for
de la Mare and Royde-Smith? The notion would explain a
lot. Yet, unlike 'The Bees' Song', 'The Honey Robbers' is one
of a number of poems handwritten onto an early typescript

of *Peacock Pie*, a typescript which contains no other poem in which one can puzzle out encoded feelings for Royde-Smith – so, while it remains very possible that this *is* secretly a poem about Royde-Smith, it would appear to be more or less the first one to be written.

But perhaps this gleeful expression of the poetic id is as much about work as it is about sex. In 1908 Sir Henry Newbolt successfully petitioned the prime minister for a one-off £200 grant for de la Mare, enough money to enable him to quit the arduous desk job at Anglo-American Oil and live in the world of letters – as much by book reviewing and acting as a publisher's reader as by writing his own books. De la Mare was no longer a slaving bee. Whatever its personal sources, I suspect the poem had its immediate origin in a dream.

The Mocking Fairy

'Won't you look out of your window, Mrs. Gill?'
    Quoth the Fairy, nidding, nodding in the garden;
'*Can't* you look out of your window, Mrs. Gill?'
    Quoth the Fairy, laughing softly in the garden;
But the air was still, the cherry boughs were still,   5
And the ivy-tod neath the empty sill,
And never from her window looked out Mrs. Gill
    On the Fairy shrilly mocking in the garden.

'What have they done with you, you poor Mrs. Gill?'
    Quoth the Fairy brightly glancing in the garden;   10
'Where have they hidden you, you poor old Mrs. Gill?'
    Quoth the Fairy dancing lightly in the garden;
But night's faint veil now wrapped the hill,
Stark 'neath the stars stood the dead-still Mill,
And out of her cold cottage never answered Mrs. Gill   15
    The Fairy mimbling, mambling in the garden.

from *Peacock Pie: A Book of Rhymes* (1913)

Why won't Mrs Gill look out of her window or come out to play? A child reader might assume it's because Mrs Gill is a dull old grown-up who doesn't want to see the fairy world that is just beyond her window. But there is a difference between someone who won't (l. 1) look out of their window and someone who can't (l. 3). As the first verse continues, everything becomes too breathless and too still, and the mocking fairy too shrill, for the scene to register as delightful. What *have* they done with Mrs Gill? Where have they hidden her? The suspicion grows that it is not only the Mill that is 'dead-still' (l. 14), a suspicion that seems to be confirmed when you bear in mind that one of the historical meanings of 'stark' given by the *Oxford English Dictionary* and used by Shakespeare was 'rigid', as in the rigidity of the dead when rigor mortis takes them.

Indeed, looking back over the poem, we can find some likely answers for the fairy's questions. The reason Mrs Gill won't look out of the window at first is because she is dying; the reason that she then can't is because she is now dead. What they have done with her? Embalmed her, probably. Where have they hidden her? In a coffin. Why does the fairy find this so funny? Well, fairies are by reputation either immortal or at least much longer lived than humans and not above mocking the afflicted. Moreover, this is probably a fairy of a particular stripe: a banshee, the fairy who in Cornwall is said to be seen outside the window of someone dying.[1]

'The Mocking Fairy' is given as the second of only two instances of 'nidding' (l. 2) in the *Oxford English Dictionary*. Still, it is a natural enough derivative from 'nid-nod', being paired up with 'nodding'. The two clearly indicate a repeated nodding motion: seeming to fall down then gaily rising again alive as ever, dance moves to poke fun at the dying and the dead. 'Mimbling' and 'mambling' (l. 16) don't appear in the *OED* at all, but their sound suggests they mean something similar to 'mumbling' or perhaps 'nimble'.

That 'The Mocking Fairy' wasn't an ordinary children's rhyme was twigged even before the poem's publication. It was one of the poems from *Peacock Pie* de la Mare sent when asked by John Middleton Murry (1889–1957) to submit poems to the journal *Rhythm* (shortly to become *The Blue Review*), where 'The Mocking Fairy' was published in March 1913. Of the poems submitted, 'The Song of the Mad Prince' was Middleton Murry's favourite; 'The Mocking Fairy', however, was the favourite of the short-story writer Katherine Mansfield (1888–1923), who was working beside Murry on the magazine at the time (Mansfield and Murry were romantically involved, and married in 1918).[2] The densely allusive 'The Song of the Mad Prince' was a natural choice for Murry, the literary highbrow who was soon to be a champion of the modernists. Mansfield's preference for 'The Mocking Fairy' was also in character. Her fiction has its own thread of cruelty, and her poetry not only contains the odd fairy but can be de la Marean to the point of pastiche. Elements of 'The Mocking Fairy' turn up in her 1917 poem 'Out in the Garden', mixed in with two other poems from *Peacock Pie*: 'Some One' and 'The Little Green Orchard'.[3] De la Mare, Mansfield and Murry met up for lunch and an afternoon of animated discussion.[4] It was to be the beginning of the friendship between Mansfield and de la Mare (See 'To K.M.').

The Song of the Mad Prince

Who said, 'Peacock Pie'?
   The old King to the sparrow:
Who said, 'Crops are ripe'?
   Rust to the harrow:
Who said, 'Where sleeps she now?   5
   Where rests she now her head,
Bathed in eve's loveliness'? –
   That's what I said.

Who said, 'Ay, mum's the word'?
   Sexton to willow: 10
Who said, 'Green dusk for dreams,
   Moss for a pillow'?
Who said, 'All Time's delight
   Hath she for narrow bed;
Life's troubled bubble broken'? –   15
   That's what I said.

from *Peacock Pie: A Book of Rhymes* (1913)

So who *did* say 'Peacock Pie'? There are more answers than you might think. De la Mare pointed out:

> this title was not in the least intended to suggest a delicacy. Indeed, I had never so much as tasted a peacock-pie, although I had frequently feasted my eyes on one in the window of Mr Pimm's restaurant in Cheapside – the bird itself, or rather its lovely but vacant plumes, seated in splendour upon the pastry's moulded upper crust. No. The book contained a piece called 'The Mad Prince'; and that begins:
>
> Who said 'Peacock Pie':
>
> Hence the spectacular title.[1]

But de la Mare had in fact said 'Peacock Pie' once before. In 'The Three Beggars' from *Songs of Childhood*, a fairy child turns the beggar man's 'crust' to 'peacock pie'.

Outside of Mr Pimm's window, peacock pie will, I suppose, look like any other pie. What is special about it – what is brutal about it – is the knowledge of how the bird within it used to appear. The peacock baked in the pie of the Mad Prince has been several things. First of all, he was Cock Robin. In his anthology of *Animal Stories*, de la Mare repeats the old version of the doleful nursery rhyme. I quote six of its fourteen verses:

> Who kill'd Cock Robin?
> I, said the sparrow,

With my bow and arrow,
I kill'd Cock Robin.

Who see him die?
    I, said the fly
    With my little eye,
And I see him die.

Who catch'd his blood?
    I, said the fish,
    With my little dish,
And I catch'd his blood.

Who made his shroud?
    I, said the beadle,
    With my little needle,
And I made his shroud.

Who shall dig his grave?
    I, said the owl,
    With my spade and showl,
And I'll dig his grave

[. . .]

And who'll toll the bell?
    I, said the bull,
    Because I can pull;
And so, Cock Robin, farewell!

135

Who killed the 'she' referred to in the poem? 'I', said the Prince?

'The Song of the Mad Prince' is a nursery rhyme. Not only is it the heir to 'Who Killed Cock Robin?', its peacock pie is baked to a similar recipe to that which in 'Sing a Song of Sixpence' sets four and twenty blackbirds in a pie before the king. Like the old nursery rhymes, these lines are at once easy to enjoy and hard to understand, but they have an intelligible gist. An old king, when presented with a sparrow on his plate, might very well say 'Peacock Pie'. Harrows break up clods of earth and remove weeds to make the ground suitable for seeds. If 'crops are ripe' (l. 3), the harrow will be idle and rusting; the rust being, as it were, the 'crop' on the harrow. The 'she' whose resting place the Mad Prince wonders about bathes in the loveliness of eve (with a small 'e', so evening not Eve's nakedness, although that sound may well be part of our sense of the word when we read the poem). One of the most important duties of a church sexton is to dig graves. People still say 'mum's the word' (l. 9) when wanting someone to keep quiet about something: in using 'mum' to mean 'silent', the poem is employing the Middle English meaning of the word. The sexton telling a tree to keep silent is dealing in grave-yard secrets, perhaps relating to the 'she' of the first verse. What the Mad Prince says in this second verse at first sounds dreamily rhapsodic, but 'Life's troubled bubble broken' (l.15), with its slightly discordant rhythm, its internal rhyme and bubble-breaking 'B' sounds, breaks both life's bubble and the poem's reverie. Coming after 'All Time's delight/ hath she for narrow bed' (ll. 13-14), it not only indicates that 'she' has died but also makes us uneasy about the fact. The last 'That's what I said' appears to indicate that the Mad Prince is as guilty as the Sparrow.

There is a literary as well as a nursery rhyme heritage behind 'The Song of the Mad Prince'. Walter Scott's 'The Pride of Youth' is included in Francis Turner Palgrave's *Golden Treasury of English Songs and Lyrics*. The copy in de la Mare's personal library has several underlinings:

> Proud Maisie is in the wood,
>   Walking so early;
> Sweet Robin sits on the bush,
>   Singing so rarely.
>
> 'Tell me, thou bonny bird,
>   When shall I marry me?'
> – 'When six braw gentlemen
>   Kirkward shall carry ye.'
>
> 'Who makes the bridal bed,
>   Birdie, say truly?'
> – 'The gray-headed sexton
>   That delves the grave duly.
>
> 'The glowworm o'er grave and stone
>   Shall light thee steady;
> The owl from the steeple sing,
>   Welcome, proud lady.'

The questions of the bird, the bringing together of romantically presented woman, sexton and grave all seem to have played their small part in shaping 'The Song of the Mad Prince'. 'The Pride of Youth' originally appeared in Scott's novel *The Heart of Midlothian*, where it is sung by Madge, who is insane and dying. Her song wishes for marriage, imagining six men as escorts on her wedding day; nevertheless, it clearly foretells a funeral with six pall-bearers. It, like William Blake's 'Mad Song', de la Mare's poem or 'Tom o' Bedlam', belongs to the genre of 'Mad Poem'.

But who is the Mad Prince? I. A. Richards identified him as the Prince of Denmark in 1926,[2] and once you decide that the Mad Prince is Shakespeare's Prince Hamlet, sort of, a number of questions resolve themselves: the 'she' in the poem must be Ophelia, who drowned where 'a willow grows aslant a brook' (*Hamlet*, Act IV Sc. 7). The sexton's 'mum's the word' relates to the hushed burial of Ophelia, whose status as a probable suicide would, in usual circumstances, have precluded her from being buried in consecrated ground. Since Hamlet visits the grave and its diggers while the grave is still being dug, the song that is the poem would presumably be sung at this time and its acknowledgement of guilt would be an acknowledgement that as the man who killed Ophelia's father, Hamlet himself was ultimately responsible for Ophelia's death.

You can, if you wish, spot other likely correspondences with *Hamlet*. The critic Filomena Aguiar de Vasconcelos has pointed out that Hamlet calls Claudius a 'very, very pajock', i.e. a metaphorical peacock (Act III, Sc. 2); thus, in telling his son to kill Claudius, Hamlet's father says 'Peacock Pie'. Since Hamlet believes 'There's a special providence in the fall of a sparrow' (Act V, Sc. 2), Hamlet is the sparrow.[3] In a similar spirit, one could add the Ghost of Hamlet's father declaring: 'I could a tale unfold whose lightest word/ Would harrow up thy soul, freeze thy young blood' (Act I, Sc. 5). The harrow in the poem might be this figurative harrow made literal and the rust upon it when crops are ripe could be interpreted as Hamlet's famously delayed revenge.

The discovery of such tucked-away references might lead one to interpret 'The Song of the Mad Prince' as, essentially, a mini-*Hamlet* or, if not that, then a poem about *Hamlet*. But that may be to miss the point. De la Mare penned a number of blank verse poems on Shakespeare characters, including 'Hamlet' and 'Ophelia', which were included in *Poems* (1906). Those were tributes and imaginative glosses. 'The Song of the Mad Prince' is something altogether richer and stranger, not Shakespeare's *Hamlet*, but *Hamlet* jumbled in dream and turned to song, a song remarkably similar to the old ballads in *Hamlet* sung not by Hamlet himself but by Ophelia in madness:

> He is dead and gone, lady,
> He is dead and gone;
> At his head a grass-green turf,
> At his heels a stone.

Act IV, Sc. 5

Who first said, 'Green dusk for dreams,/ Moss for a pillow' (ll. 11–12)? Not Hamlet.

In his letter to de la Mare of 15 October 1919, Thomas Hardy writes that 'The Song of the Mad Prince' has for him 'a meaning almost too intense to speak of'. The editors of Hardy's letters gloss this with the suggestion that Hardy seems to have associated the poem with the death of his first wife.[4] 'The Song of the Mad Prince' was very probably the last poem written for *Peacock Pie* (it appears in none of the lists of poems prior to publication) and was therefore written when the liaison with Naomi Royde-Smith was at its most intense and de la Mare's marriage was at its lowest ebb. 'The Song of the Mad Prince' is by no means an autobiographical poem, but it may be that if the poem recalled Hardy's feelings of remorse and self-reproach towards his first wife, it was because it was a poem which has a husband's guilt as one of its emotional spurs.

For All the Grief

For all the grief I have given with words
    May now a few clear flowers blow,
In the dust, and the heat, and the silence of birds,
      Where the friendless go.

For the thing unsaid that heart asked of me   5
    Be a dark, cool water calling – calling
To the footsore, benighted, solitary,
      Where the shadows are falling.

O, be beauty for all my blindness,
    A moon in the air where the weary wend,   10
And dews burdened with loving-kindness
      In the dark of the end.

from *Motley and Other Poems* (1918)

'For All the Grief' was written in a sketchbook which also contains drawings by Ralph Hodgson, who had plans to illustrate some of de la Mare's rhymes for children, as well as doodlings by de la Mare's son Colin. Other poems in the book – the love-forsaken 'Alone', the terrifying children's rhyme 'The Little Creature' – find de la Mare in a very dark frame of mind. The reasons for this are not hard to fathom: not only was it now wartime but de la Mare was in Guy's Hospital in London, recovering from the appendectomy he'd had on 12 November 1914.[1] At a time when there was no free health care he was also badly off, his job as reader for William Heinemann having ended at the beginning of the war. What's more, his romantic relationship with Naomi Royde-Smith was in its last days.

'For All the Grief', however, dwells not on the speaker's misfortune but on the greater suffering of others. In the sketchbook, the poem is dated 23 November 1914. On Thursday, 19 November, de la Mare had been visited by Rupert Brooke.[2] The two hadn't known each other well, but Brooke had evidently taken a liking to de la Mare, writing to Edward Marsh, mutual friend and editor of the *Georgian Poetry* anthologies, from Tahiti in 1914: 'What do the jolly people all do? I want to belong to the same club as de la Mare. Where does de la Mare go?'[3] Brooke, by the time of the November visit, had recently returned from fighting at the fall of Antwerp and was awaiting his next posting. He was at this time full of the plight of the Belgian refugees, which he describes to another correspondent:

They put their goods on carts, barrows, perambulators, anything. Often the carts had no horses, and they just stayed there in the street, waiting for a miracle. There were all the country refugees too [. . .] I'll never forget that white-faced, endless procession in the night, pressed to let the military – us – pass, crawling forward at some hundred yards an hour, quite hopeless the old men crying, and the women with hard drawn faces.[4]

Brooke would, I imagine, have told similar tales to de la Mare.

Although Brooke seems to have promised de la Mare another visit, on returning home from seeing him he discovered he had received his next posting, to Portsmouth.[5] Brooke wrote to de la Mare from the Royal Army Barracks on the twentieth, wishing first of all to tell de la Mare how 'I loved your poem on the war in *The Times* in August'. The poem, which appeared in the *Times Literary Supplement* on 27 August, a week or so after Brooke had decided to enlist, was 'Happy England'.[6] The last three stanzas read:

> Remember happy England: keep
>   For her bright cause thy latest breath;
> Her peace that long hath lulled to sleep,
>   May now exact the sleep of death.
>
> Her woods and wilds, her loveliness,
>   With harvest now are richly at rest;
> Safe in her isled securities,
>   Thy children's heaven is her breast.

O what a deep, contented night
    The sun from out her Eastern seas
Would bring the dust which in her sight
    Had given its all for these!

The poem, which de la Mare was to exclude from his *Collected Poems* (1942), has common ground with the war sonnets Brooke was writing, particularly 'I. Peace', which begins 'Now, God be thanked Who has matched us with His hour,/ And caught our youth, and wakened us from sleeping,' and 'V. The Soldier'.[7] In his letter of 20 November Brooke shares his current state of mind: 'We're waiting here for the invasion: ready to go off at any hour of day or night. It's queer that the Admiralty seem so certain of it happening. I've a kind of horror at the idea of England being invaded, as of some virginity violated. But I'd enjoy fighting in England. How one could die!'[8]

'For All the Grief" makes a strong break with the hallucinatory symbolism and word magic of *Peacock Pie* and *The Listeners* for a much plainer, more direct style. Rather than delighting in words, it has turned to question them. The title phrase might mean 'because of all the grief' or 'in spite of it'; both make sense, though the latter seems more likely. The word 'clear' (l. 2) is used in its older meaning of 'free from murk'; 'blow' (l. 2) here means 'bloom'. The metre mirrors the syntax, making a delicate pattern of call and response; it also results in some strong mimetic effects, including the weary slog of anapaests in the poem's third line before its much shorter, friendless fourth. De la Mare has lost none of his great skill, but he has suddenly become a very different sort of poet.

Fare Well

When I lie where shades of darkness
Shall no more assail mine eyes,
Nor the rain make lamentation
    When the wind sighs;
How will fare the world whose wonder   5
Was the very proof of me?
Memory fades, must the remembered
    Perishing be?

Oh, when this my dust surrenders
Hand, foot, lip, to dust again,   10
May these loved and loving faces
    Please other men!
May the rusting harvest hedgerow
Still the Traveller's Joy entwine,
And as happy children gather   15
    Posies once mine.

Look thy last on all things lovely,
Every hour. Let no night
Seal thy sense in deathly slumber
    Till to delight   20
Thou have paid thy utmost blessing;
Since that all things thou wouldst praise

Beauty took from those who loved them
   In other days.

from *Motley and Other Poems* (1918)

According to Theresa Whistler, 'Fare Well' was written while de la Mare was staying with Sir Henry and Lady Margaret Newbolt at Netherhampton in Wiltshire in either February 1915 or February 1916.[1] The earlier date is the more probable; not only is the vein of 'Fare Well' similar to that of 'For All the Grief' but it feels like a poem by someone who has recently had a close brush with death. Moreover, as he was recovering his health in February 1915, de la Mare was also reading the final issue of the journal *New Numbers*, in order to write a book review for the *Times Literary Supplement*. That issue was the first place Rupert Brooke's war sonnets were published, and de la Mare's review of 11 March praises them very highly. Of 'V. The Soldier', he writes: 'No passion for glory is here, no bitterness, no gloom, only a happy, clear-sighted, all-surrendering love'.[2] De la Mare quoted the whole of the poem, which begins:

> If I should die, think only this of me:
>   That there's some corner of a foreign field
> That is for ever England. There shall be
>   In that rich earth a richer dust concealed;
> A dust whom England bore, shaped, made aware,
>   Gave, once, her flowers to love, her ways to roam,[3]

This review brought the poem to the attention of the Dean of St Paul's Cathedral, who proceeded to repeat it in an Easter sermon that, when reported by *The Times*, caused a rush of interest in Brooke and his verse.[4]

On 10 March, Brooke, who presumably had little inkling

of the role his friend was taking in the process that would make him and his work famous, made de la Mare his heir and literary executor alongside the poets Wilfrid Gibson and Lascelles Abercrombie, reckoning: 'If I can set them free, to any extent to write the poetry and plays and books they want to, my death will bring more gain than loss.'[5] Brooke's books quickly went on to sell a huge number of copies, and the bequest played a key role in ensuring de la Mare's financial security in the years ahead.

Brooke died of sepsis from an infected mosquito bite on 23 April 1915 while on his way to fight at Gallipoli; he was buried on the Greek island of Skyros. Thereafter, de la Mare would become something of an ambassador for Brooke's legacy. Having been turned down for military service on the grounds of being 'over age' and 'not hale', de la Mare would travel to America in 1916 to accept a prize from Yale University on Brooke's behalf.[6]

De la Mare did write a few war poems, including some far less blithe in the face of war's slaughter than 'Happy England'. Nevertheless, these poems were not especially suited to de la Mare's poetic gifts and nor were they the product of any direct experience of battle. De la Mare's keenness to serve eventually found war work behind a government desk in 1917, helping to introduce and then administer rationing.

The great poems de la Mare wrote in the war are, rather than war poems, poems of peace. The words of 'Fare Well' provide a generous and pacific alternative to poems like 'The Soldier' – its genuinely self-abnegating sentiment, acceptance of death and nobility of tone are not in the service of country or even the self, but of a pacific, nature- and future-loving blessing. It is the strength of the poem's sentiment as much as its delicate lyric beauty that has made 'Fare Well' one of de la Mare's best-loved poems. When the St Lucian poet Derek Walcott appeared on BBC Radio 4's *Desert Island Discs* in 1992, he was asked: 'If you could take one other poet's work . . . who would you take?' and answered: 'I'm very, very haunted by de la Mare's poem "Fare Well" [. . .] a magical writer.' Pressed to enlarge on why it was so great, Walcott answered: 'It's the whole thing – it's like nothing belongs to you in this world and you leave it behind and the commemoration of that, I think, is exquisite.'[7] 'Fare Well' was the poem that de la Mare would haltingly speak on his deathbed, having been asked to recite it by his son Richard.[8]

The poem's title is not 'Farewell', but 'Fare Well'; rather than merely offering a 'goodbye', it also wishes others to 'proceed' or 'survive' well, to 'travel well' through life (the older meaning of 'to fare' being 'to travel'). Countless poems have imaged death as a place of darkness. Here, though, we have a state where 'shades of darkness/ Shall no more assail [i.e. assault] mine eyes' (ll. 1–2), for the shades of darkness we witness in life will no more be seen. After death, others may sigh and lament awhile; nature herself may even seem to do so too in wind and rain. For the deceased, however, sounds of sighing and lamentation, whether human or natural, will no longer be heard.

Having set down how he himself may fare in this state of non-being, de la Mare begins to think of the world in his absence, a world 'whose wonder' (l. 5) has been the true 'proof', not merely 'the confirmation' but also 'the test' of his own existence. John Bayley interprets lines 7–8 to mean that as the memory of things fades it greatly cheers de la Mare 'to think of them being enjoyed by others – especially children'.[9] This seems the primary meaning. But, given the sentiments of the preceding lines, it is also possible to interpret the 'Memory' (l. 7) as belonging to those who will remain after the speaker has gone. The question, 'must the remembered/ Perishing be?' (ll. 7–8), would then be carefully unspecific over the identity of 'the remembered': to judge from the poem thus far, one would assume it to be the speaker when he is dead; from the content to come, it would become the things of the world of which he is mindful.

The word 'dust' (l. 9) indicates the body which, on dying, surrenders itself to literal dust, as in Genesis 3:19: 'for dust thou *art*, and unto dust shalt thou return'. 'Hand, foot, lip, to dust' (l. 10) recalls 'Of hand, of foot, of lip' in Shakespeare's Sonnet 106, 'When in the Chronicle of Wasted Time'.[10] Those 'loved and loving faces' (l. 11) are the faces of loved ones, though given what follows in the stanza, the phrase may also include the 'faces' of the loved things of the natural world. The harvest hedgerow is 'rusting' rather than the more-expected 'rustling' (l. 13), that is, it is turning red and brown, a sign of nature's own passing away. 'Traveller's Joy' (l. 14) or clematis is a fragrant white-flowered climbing plant common to English hedgerows and still in flower after harvest time, its name signifying the joy it gives to wayfarers, a plant that helps them 'fare well'. Its hairy appearance after flowering gives the plant its other name, old man's beard. Here it blooms 'as happy children' (l. 15) gather flowers – at the same time as the dying and rusting of the leaves of the hedgerow – though it is also making children as happy as the speaker once was. While the primary sense of 'posies' (l. 16) is bunches of flowers, 'posy' can also mean a line of verse. The word is also similar to 'poesy', an old word for poetry. There is an ancient tradition that connects the gathering of poetry with the gathering of flowers, which is the literal meaning of the word 'anthology', hence the title of Lord Wavell's collection *Other Men's Flowers*.

At the start of the last stanza, the poem exhorts speaker and audience to relish the world as if always about to leave it. The words are 'Let no night' (l. 18) rather than 'let not night', so it is not a straightforward euphemism for death that is being referred to but other, metaphorical nights (whether bringing death or merely like death) that might seal the sense in slumber and prevent appreciation of the loveliness of the world before one has given delight in it 'utmost blessing' (l. 21). When asked by the Public Orator at Oxford University, who was translating these words into Latin, de la Mare confirmed 'Beauty' as being the object and not the subject of the last two lines.[11] If so, their meaning is that 'those who once loved all the things that you would praise now took beauty from those things in other days'. Nevertheless, this is an occasion where de la Mare's use of inversion creates a satisfying ambiguity. If we read 'Beauty' as the subject, a personified Beauty took away these things from others who loved them in other days and the poem would equate beauty with transience, which is, after all, one of the poem's themes. The poem's last two lines once more echo Sonnet 106, this time its closing couplet:

'For we, which now behold these present days/ Have eyes to wonder, but lack tongues to praise'. And indeed, the praise of past and, above all, present wonder in 'Fare Well' as a whole can be read as an eloquent response to Shakespeare's own reflections on their relationship to beauty and transience.

'Fare Well' is arranged in seemingly regular, near identical stanza shapes – the fourth and eighth lines of a stanza, are, for example, always four syllables long, yet there is a subtle pattern of metrical variation and substitution throughout. One finely judged pattern is the gradual changing of the poem's apparent metre. You *could* begin the opening line by stressing 'When', but few people would, and most would instead start with two unstressed syllables and could quite easily continue stressing the opening of each of the stanza's long and short lines in the same manner until reaching its last two lines, which require one to begin with a stressed syllable: ('*Mem*ory (l. 7) and '*Per*ishing (l. 8)). In the second stanza, the stressing of that first syllable is subtly promoted: even if one doesn't stress 'Oh' (l. 9) – though, I think, most would – one certainly has to stress 'Hand' (l. 10), the effect of which is to make the reader bring an affirmative stress to 'May' (l. 11). By the time we reach the third stanza, few readers would not give 'Look' (l. 17) a resolute stress, and all would stress the 'Ev' in 'Every' (l. 18) as well as 'Seal' (l. 19). The metre has moved from pondering to resolve.

The poet and classical scholar A. E. Housman (1859–1936) first came across 'Fare Well' when its second stanza was reproduced in a newspaper book review. Line 13 was written as 'May the rustling harvest hedgerow'. Housman reported that he guessed at once that the poet of the rest of the stanza could not have written a word as predictable as 'rustling' and that it must have been a misprint. He then, he states, quickly worked out the right word ('rusting'). Housman subsequently used the example to justify his interventionist style of editing classical texts.[12] His own poem 'Tell Me Not Here, It Needs Not Saying' not only strongly echoes 'Fare Well', but, as John Bayley points out, also appears to be offering de la Mare's poem a less happy 'answer'.[13]

The Scribe

What lovely things
   Thy hand hath made:
The smooth-plumed bird
   In its emerald shade,
The seed of the grass,   5
   The speck of stone
Which the wayfaring ant
   Stirs – and hastes on!

Though I should sit
   By some tarn in thy hills,   10
Using its ink
   As the spirit wills
To write of Earth's wonders,
   Its live, willed things,
Flit would the ages   15
   On soundless wings
Ere unto Z
   My pen drew nigh;
Leviathan told,
   And the honey-fly: 20
And still would remain
   My wit to try –
My worn reeds broken,
   The dark tarn dry,

All words forgotten –
Thou, Lord, and I.

from *Motley and Other Poems* (1918)

In another poem of thanksgiving written against the backdrop of the war, the scribe's faith in how the world outstrips human representation may have something of Plato's distrust of the imitative arts, but also reflects how the war had made words, the counters of de la Mare's craft, seem both unreliable and not very useful. Yet, unlike 'For All the Grief', that limitation of art and language has here become something to rejoice in. This is a religious poem, but one not written *in propria persona*: the scribe must be a medieval copyist, probably a monk addressing the greater scribe, who, ultimately, is the Creator Himself.

The images of the first stanza are like the illuminations in a manuscript: the contrast between the first and second stanzas is between the primary creation 'Thy hand hath made' (l. 2) and the secondary creation of writing down 'Earth's wonders' (l. 13). The 'emerald shade' (l. 4) must refer to the shade of leaves. The seed of grass and the stone stirred by the ant (ll. 5–8) is somewhat reminiscent of William Blake's desire in his 'Auguries of Innocence' to 'To see a World in a Grain of Sand/ And a Heaven in a Wild Flower', but de la Mare had a peculiar affinity for the contemplation of tiny things.[1] 'The Fly' in *Songs of Childhood* reflects:

> How large unto the tiny fly
>   Must little things appear! –
> A rosebud like a feather bed,
> Its prickle like a spear;
>
> A dewdrop like a looking-glass,
> A hair like golden wire . . .

In his 1921 novel *Memoirs of a Midget*, de la Mare's appreciation of things small would be writ large.

A 'tarn' (l. 10) is a small, glacier-formed lake or pond in the hills or mountains, and 'its ink' (l. 11) is its dark water. John Lingard glosses this with reference to the title poem of de la Mare's *Memory* (1938): here, memory has 'tarn-dark eyes', a fact that leads Lingard to equate the tarn with memory or inspiration.[2] But I wonder if de la Mare's point isn't more easily guessable. Tarn water, though it appears ink-dark and huge in quantity, won't serve to write anything legible. Isn't this a more straightforward image of the delights and ultimate futility of authorship in the face of creation?

The imagery also calls to mind that of Romantic poets. In the 'Introduction' to William Blake's *Songs of Innocence and of Experience*, a child on a cloud asks the narrator to:

> . . . sit thee down and write
> In a book that all may read –
> So he vanish'd from my sight.
> And I pluck'd a hollow reed.
>
> And I made a rural pen,
> And I stain'd the water clear,
> And I wrote my happy songs
> Every child may joy to hear.[3]

On Keats's tombstone are the words: 'Here lies One Whose Name was writ in Water.' The 'honey-fly' (l. 20) is an old name for the honey bee.

To E.T.: 1917

You sleep too well – too far away,
    For sorrowing word to soothe or wound;
Your very quiet seems to say
    How longed-for a peace you have found.

Else, had not death so lured you on,   5
    You would have grieved – 'twixt joy and fear –
To know how my small loving son
    Had wept for you, my dear.

From *Motley and Other Poems* (1918)

Edward Thomas died at the Battle of Arras on 9 April 1917. News reached de la Mare within a week, and 'To E.T.: 1917', which first appeared in the slim 1917 volume *The Sunken Garden*, must have been written shortly afterwards.

For all sorts of little reasons – and for bigger ones, such as de la Mare's preoccupation with Naomi Royde-Smith and Thomas's friendship with Robert Frost – the relationship between Thomas and de la Mare cooled a little in its later years. Nevertheless, the friendship was a long way from being broken, and my impression is that by the time Thomas left for France, the two were closer than they had been for a while. Their correspondence continued to the end, and 'To E.T.: 1917' is almost a last letter to the man who signed off letters with 'E.T.'. Yet when de la Mare wrote letters, he wrote 'My dear Thomas' rather than 'To E.T.', signing his own name 'WJdlM'.[1] In this poem, the standard formula 'My dear' becomes a sincere endearment, and is placed at the end of the address. Nor is this the only aspect of the poem in which the shape of de la Mare's grief alters expected formulae. 'You sleep too well' recalls the familiar wish of the epitaph writer that the dead should 'rest in peace' or the fond falsehood that declares how the body in the grave is not dead but only sleeping (de la Mare may also be recalling John Skelton's 'With lullay, lullay lyke a childe/ Though slepyst too long; thou art begylde', a poem more clearly alluded to in '*Sotto Voce*'). But the wish for Thomas to rest in peace here comes only from Thomas; there is no such wish from de la Mare.

De la Mare's review of *An Annual of New Poetry*, which appeared in the *Saturday Westminster Gazette* on 28 April 1917, was both de la Mare's first public elegy for Thomas and the first place where he publicly discussed Thomas's verse. The article contains two quotations referring to sleep, one from Thomas's 'Roads':

> They are lonely
> While we sleep, lonelier
> For lack of the traveller
> Who is now a dream only.[2]

And one from Thomas's last poem, 'Lights Out':

> I have come to the borders of sleep,
> The unfathomable deep
> Forest where all must lose
> Their way

The review also refers to Thomas's 'Beauty', a poem de la Mare introduces by noting how to a melancholy nature such as Thomas's, 'Earthly existence may seem nothing but a cage'. De la Mare's withholding of sleep runs contrary to the sentiments of his own 'Happy England' and its more positive portrayal of the 'sleep of death'. Nowhere in 'To E.T.: 1917' is there any indication that Thomas has died fighting for his country and the cause that de la Mare had so strongly advocated. It seems no coincidence that Robert Frost's own later elegy to Thomas, 'To E.T.' should borrow and trim de la Mare's title and make a point of honouring Thomas as a soldier-poet.

De la Mare's use of 'wound' (l. 2) is informed by the belief that Thomas died woundless from the concussive blast of an exploding shell (Jean Moorcroft Wilson's recent biography of Thomas makes a strong case that he was, in fact, hit by a shell and that the story of his woundless death was invented as a comfort for his widow, Helen).[3] The phrases 'longed-for a peace' (l. 4) and 'death so lured you on' (l. 5) indicate not the self-sacrifice of a patriotic warrior, but something closer to suicide. De la Mare knew Thomas's depressions and his strong thoughts of taking his own life well; indeed, he had talked Thomas out of killing himself.[4] Not only was Thomas over the age of conscription; his decision to accept a commission in the Royal Garrison Artillery, with inevitable frontline service and likely death, could be seen to have suicidal as well as selfless and patriotic motivations.

In his foreword to Thomas's *Collected Poems* (1920), de la Mare writes:

> To read 'The Trumpet', 'Tears', or 'This is No Case of Petty Right or Wrong' is to realise the brave spirit that compelled him to fling away the safety which without the least loss of honour he might have accepted, and to go back to his men, and his guns, and death. These poems show, too, that he was doubly homesick, for this and for another world, no less clearly than they show how intense a happiness was the fruition of his livelong hope and desire to prove himself a poet.[5]

'To E.T.: 1917' is an angry and unreconciled poem: 'you

would have grieved' (l. 6), postulates another, less death-lured Thomas, who would grieve for the grief his own death caused. And while de la Mare doesn't go so far as to mention Thomas's widow and children, whom de la Mare was to help, not least by being instrumental in securing a Civil List pension for Helen Thomas, he does mention his own son – either the older Richard, who would have known Thomas better, or Colin, Thomas's godson. De la Mare's own loss is alluded to only in 'my dear' (l. 8). But those two words betray a huge sense of loss. De la Mare would later write of Thomas: 'Nobody like him was in this world that I have ever had the happiness to meet . . . So when he died, a ghost of one's self went away with him.'[6]

Sotto Voce

To Edward Thomas

The haze of noon wanned silver-grey
The soundless mansion of the sun:
The air made visible in his ray,
Like molten glass from furnace run,
Quivered o'er heat-baked turf and stone   5
And the flower of the gorse burned on –
Burned softly as gold of a child's fair hair
Along each spiky spray, and shed
Almond-like incense in the air
Whereon our senses fed.   10

At foot – a few sparse harebells: blue
And still as were the friend's dark eyes
That dwelt on mine, transfixèd through
With sudden ecstatic surmise.

'Hst!' he cried softly, smiling, and lo,   15
Stealing amidst that maze gold-green,
I heard a whispering music flow
From guileful throat of bird, unseen: –
So delicate the straining ear
Scarce carried its faint syllabling   20
Into a heart caught up to hear

That inmost pondering
Of bird–like self with self. We stood,
In happy trance–like solitude,
Hearkening a lullay grieved and sweet –   25
As when on isle uncharted beat
'Gainst coral at the palm-tree's root,
With brine-clear, snow-white foam afloat,
The wailing, not of water or wind –
A husht, far, wild, divine lament,   30
When Prospero his wizardry bent
Winged Ariel to bind . . .

Then silence, and o'er-flooding noon.
I raised my head; smiled too. And he –
Moved his great hand, the magic gone –   35
Gently amused to see
My ignorant wonderment. He sighed.
'It was a nightingale,' he said,
'That *sotto voce* cons the song
He'll sing when dark is spread;   40
And Night's vague hours are sweet and long,
And we are laid abed.'

from *The Veil and Other Poems* (1921)

The phrase *sotto voce* is Italian and its literal meaning is 'under voice'. Written on a piece of music, the term is a direction to sing very quietly.

In the poem, Edward Thomas alerts de la Mare to the 'whispering music' (l. 17) of a nightingale. This is what is now termed the nightingale's 'subsong', which at the time was referred to as its 'whisper song' and is most associated with young birds learning their song from a tutor bird. Nightingale subsong is quieter than adult song and also contains a different pattern of notes, with more chattering and rattles.[1]

The presence of 'harebells' (l. 11) would suggest that '*Sotto Voce*' is set in July or August, so towards the end of the nightingale's residence in England and after the adult males would typically have finished their nightly songs of courtship. I would guess that the event described in the poem happened during one of the de la Mare family's summer stays in West Harting in 1909, 1910 or 1911, when de la Mare and Thomas would regularly take walks together. It is hot noon, under a white sky. The middle of the day has 'wanned' (l. 1) (paled) to take on a lunar look: mansions are stages in the moon's progress, rather than the sun's. 'The soundless mansion of the sun' (l. 2) could also be a description of one of de la Mare's old houses.

The comparison of the gorse blossom with the 'gold of a child's fair hair' (l. 7) recalls Laura in Christina Rossetti's *Goblin Market*. Enchanted by the goblin's call to taste their deadly fruit, she declares:

> 'I have no copper in my purse,
> I have no silver either,

167

And all my gold is on the furze
That shakes in windy weather
Above the rusty heather.'
'You have much gold upon your head,'
They answer'd all together:
'Buy from us with a golden curl.'[2]

'Furze' here is a synonym for gorse. In *Come Hither*, de la Mare quotes Thomas's 'If I Should Ever By Chance' with its line 'But if she finds a blossom on furze', a poem which also seems to have *Goblin Market* at the back of its mind. Commenting on Thomas's poem, de la Mare notes how 'As a matter of fact, the scent of the furze-blossoms is not exactly sweet, but nutlike and aromatic', before quoting the nature writer W. H. Hudson:

The gorse is most fragrant at noon, when the sun shines brightest and hottest. At such an hour when I approach a thicket of furze, the wind blowing from it, I am always tempted to cast myself down on the grass to lie for an hour drinking in the odour. The effect is to make me languid; to wish to lie till I sleep and live again in dreams in another world, in a vast open-air cathedral where a great festival of ceremony is perpetually in progress, and acolytes, in scores and hundreds with beautiful bright faces, in flame yellow and orange surplices, are ever and ever coming toward me, swinging their censers until I am ready to swoon in that heavenly incense![3]

The words 'sudden ecstatic surmise' (l. 14) recall John Keats's 'On First Looking into Chapman's Homer':

> Or like stout Cortez when with eagle eyes
> He star'd at the Pacific – and all his men
> Look'd at each other with a wild surmise –
> Silent, upon a peak in Darien.[4]

The other Keats poem that de la Mare clearly has in mind here, even if he doesn't explicitly allude to it, is 'Ode to a Nightingale'.

When Thomas first sent de la Mare his verse in 1915, de la Mare, though appreciative of some of the poems, thought Thomas had 'gone wrong over metre sometimes'.[5] Nevertheless, de la Mare was to become a vigorous public champion of Thomas's poetry and its innovations in the months and years after the latter's death. In an article in the *Times Literary Supplement* on 18 October 1917, de la Mare justifies Thomas's metrical experiments by comparing them to a nightingale practising its song:

> It is a poetry that not only breaks away from poetic
> convention, into a verse in which the rhymes are
> the faintest of echoes, the metre at times scarcely
> distinguishable, and the form as insubstantial as a
> ghost's, but much of it is 'about' what most poets leave
> unremarked, or, at any rate, unrecorded. We listen
> to a kind of monologue, like that of one of his own
> nightingales softly practising over its song, as though

in utmost secrecy we were overhearing a man talking
quietly to himself, or to a friend strangely silent and
understanding, pouring out his reveries, ruminations,
remembrances. Yet these are not remembrances only
of what has happened in the past, but of what is almost
insupportably real and near and present, taking the aspect
of the past on the eve of a long farewell.[6]

This is the germ of what de la Mare would convey in 'Sotto
Voce'. The poem celebrates what united Thomas and de la
Mare as well as what divided them, including the verse of
Keats, Christina Rossetti and Shakespeare, and a mystical at-
tachment to the beguiling qualities of birdsong.[7] Nonetheless,
the two poets appears to be cast into their different types:
Thomas as the whispering poet of carefully observed nature,
de la Mare as the singer of reverie and dreams. According
to Prospero in Act I Scene 2 of Shakespeare's The Tempest,
Ariel's binding took place when Prospero released him from
the pine tree in which Ariel had been bound by Sycorax. De
la Mare may also have in mind scenes from the play featur-
ing Ariel. In his introduction to an edition of Shakespeare's
songs, de la Mare writes how Ariel 'decoys Ferdinand [. . .]
within sight of Miranda, with his "Come unto these yellow
sands" [. . .] Ferdinand speaks sorrowfully and *sotto voce* of his
father, and Ariel's "Full fathom five," is his mocking reply.'[8]
But de la Mare's Ariel has as much to do with his own dreams
of desert islands as Shakespeare's.

In his introduction to *A Choice of De la Mare's Verse*,
W. H. Auden, whose fantasia on *The Tempest*, *The Sea and the*

Mirror, owes something to '*Sotto Voce*', declares how in each poet 'dwells an Ariel, who sings, and a Prospero, who comprehends' but that in every poem, and sometimes in a poet, one will have the upper hand. De la Mare, like Thomas Campion, is an 'Ariel-dominated poet'.[9] For an example of the more rational Prospero, Auden gives the Wordsworth of *The Prelude*. '*Sotto Voce*' doesn't find de la Mare casting himself as Ariel, but both the nightingale and by implication Edward Thomas, the future poet, are presented as Ariel-taming Prosperos.

'*Sotto Voce*' calls to mind a number of instances of memorable 'unseen' birds in Thomas's poetry and prose, particularly 'The Unknown Bird', with its call 'As if a cock crowed past the edge of the world,/ As if the bird or I were in a dream' and its description of Thomas's past listening self that (in the manner of Ariel) is 'Light as that bird wandering beyond my shore'.[10] 'Lullay' and indeed 'lully', 'lulla' or 'Lulley' are all to be found in poems included by de la Mare in *Behold, This Dreamer!* All are variants of the soothing refrain from old lullabies, and it is from this refrain that the word 'lullaby' derives: a lulling sound, its appearance in 'The Coventry Carol' of the sixteenth century is its best known. The word is spelled 'lullay' in de la Mare's transcription of John Skelton's 'With lullay, lullay lyke a childe/ Thou slepyst to long; thou art begylde', as a refrain used by a false woman to sooth her lover to sleep.[11] The nightingale in this poem is described as 'guileful' (l. 18); it is, like the false lover in Skelton's poem, soothing to sleep in order to betray. The call to sleep is, as it is in 'To E.T.: 1917' , a call to death, a promise to him to be in full song come nightfall.

Titmouse

If you would happy company win,
Dangle a palm-nut from a tree,
Idly in green to sway and spin,
Its snow-pulped kernel for bait; and see
    A nimble titmouse enter in.   5

Out of earth's vast unknown of air,
Out of all summer, from wave to wave,
He'll perch, and prank his feathers fair,
Jangle a glass-clear wildering stave,
    And take his commons there –   10

This tiny son of life; this spright,
By momentary Human sought,
Plume will his wing in the dappling light,
Clash timbrel shrill and gay –
And into Time's enormous Nought,
    Sweet-fed, will flit away.   15

from *The Veil and Other Poems* (1921)

The titmouse is not an actual mouse but a small bird with a mouse-like tail: a tit or tomtit, a popular visitor to England's bird tables. In *Come Hither*, de la Mare writes:

> to anybody who cares to watch a living nimble delightful thing at all, even a glimpse of a Long-tailed Tit is an event. To see *one*, indeed, is usually to see a complete family. You hear their small shrill calling, look up, and lo! – scattering from tree to tree they flit, with their loose, grey, ruffish feathers, small hooked beaks, and long slim tails, searching for caterpillars and tiny beetles, clinging to spray or twig wrong-side-up and upside-down, noisy, merry, alert. And then – all gone, vanished, fled! Into some other green garden – as momentary as a rainbow.[1]

In 'Titmouse', de la Mare is using the word 'company' (l. 1) in line with its etymological meaning: those one shares bread with. Other pieces of the poem's vocabulary may be technically archaisms but are, nonetheless, perfectly chosen. To 'prank' (l. 8) is to dress or decorate, a word associated with human dress – so not the same thing as 'to preen'. To 'wilder' is to go or lead astray – a 'wildering stave' (l. 9) would be a wandering piece of music; the word is presumably chosen for its relationship to 'wildness', though a wildness in terms of that emblem of human culture, the musical stave. To take one's 'commons' (l. 10) is to eat food shared by a community (originally of monks, nuns or scholars), the word here strongly implying a commonality between human and bird. A 'spright' (l. 11) is a sprite. The sense of the supernatural, but also the sense of its being souled, is pertinent; the old spelling also conveys a sense of 'sprightly'. A timbrel is a tambourine-like instrument, familiar from the King James Bible.

In his introduction to *Animal Stories*, de la Mare writes:

Watch a 'wild' animal, as far as you can, following its own ways and habits. Imagine what a joy it would be if, in wood or field or garden, a rich and genuine friendliness were the rule between yourself and it; and if it could, as far as nature allows, share your mind to the extent to which, as far as nature and a generous heart allows you, you *might* learn to share *its*. [. . .]Of one thing [. . .] we can be positively certain: namely, that, with very few exceptions – a tiger in the kitchen say, a boa constrictor in one's bed, or a scorpion in one's shoe (unusual little experiences all three) – we shall never regret having spared the life of the least of living creatures, or be sorry for having shown kindness to one in need.[2]

'Titmouse' has a significant place in contemporary thinking on animal rights, having been quoted in a much-discussed passage in an influential 1978 essay by the philosopher Cora Diamond.[3] Diamond is struck by the phrase 'this tiny son of life' (l. 11) and the way the titmouse is presented as a fellow creature, stressing how this is connected with the bird's appearing out of 'earth's vast unknown of air', and flitting off into 'Time's enormous Nought'. It is this response to 'animals as our fellows in mortality, in life on this earth' that Diamond finds instructive for thinking on humans' relationship with other animals more generally.[4]

Good-Bye

The last of last words spoken is, Good-bye –
The last dismantled flower in the weed-grown hedge,
The last thin rumour of a feeble bell far ringing,
The last blind rat to spurn the mildewed rye.

A hardening darkness glasses the haunted eye,   5
Shines into nothing the watcher's burnt-out candle,
Wreathes into scentless nothing the wasting incense,
Faints in the outer silence the hunting-cry.

Love of its muted music breathes no sigh,
Thought in her ivory tower gropes in her spinning,   10
Toss on in vain the whispering trees of Eden,
Last of all last words spoken is, Good-bye.

from *The Veil and Other Poems* (1921)

'Good-Bye' is a list of last things, made after the last things have gone: the last language, the last flower, the last bell, the last rat giving up on the inedible rye, the last sight, scent and sound, the last music, the last thought. On its publication in *The Veil* in 1921, it must have seemed a desolate leave-taking breathed over the post-war wasteland. Yet the poem's sense of aftermath dates from before that: a very slightly different version of the poem had been intended for inclusion in *The Listeners*. Indeed, its sense of things is the abject version of what we find in a poem such as 'The Bells': not the last, richly savoured reverberations and after-echoes of a heavenly sound, but the echoes and after-images of the world thinned to its final vestiges. 'Good-Bye' is, in a way, a counterpart to the rust-armoured knight of skin and bone who goes charging off into the void in 'The Song of Finis', the last rhyme of *Peacock Pie*. Quite how despairing a poem you take it to be ultimately depends on how you take its title, 'Good-Bye' being a contraction of 'God be with ye'.

'Good-Bye' is, as Eric Ormsby points out, an example of de la Mare at his most rhetorical. The poem makes extensive use of the rhetorical devices of 'anaphora' (the repetition of words in successive clauses, as when 'The last' appears at the beginning of each line of the first verse) and 'anastrophe' (the inverting of the usual word order of subject, verb and object). De la Mare's use of anastrophe has come in for a lot of criticism. Its employment risks sounding convoluted and old-fashioned, and can leave the reader needlessly uncertain of the intended meaning of a line. On the publication of *The Veil*, even de la Mare's friend and admirer Forrest

Reid was questioning his fondness for it: in his letter to de la Mare of 13 December 1921, Reid tells him that he was in the habit of swapping around subject and verb merely because he liked to do so.[1] Yet, as Reid conceded in his next letter, if employed occasionally, the device can be used to achieve a particular effect.[2] A stronger argument in favour of this and of how other verbal peculiarities of de la Mare can often be successful is put by the philosopher and critic Owen Barfield when he declares: 'the liberties taken by de la Mare in the use of language were in fact a *sine qua non* of his achievement'.[3] Eric Ormsby's recent reassessment returns to something like Barfield's view of the matter. For Ormsby, the rhetorical devices in 'Good-Bye' link with the poem's intricate prosody (one doesn't associate such music as one finds here with the iambic pentameter, but de la Mare has managed to write a pentameter whose feet are very rarely iambs) to function like 'cunningly interlaced vines over the dark mouth of a pit'.[4] One might add that not only can the inversion of verb and subject place an important emphasis on the verb (as in 'All That's Past') but that the ambiguity created by anastrophe can, when handled with sufficient care, create a rich bifurcation of meaning.

In 'Good-Bye', the use of anastrophe is certainly ambiguous. Is 'Good-bye' the 'last word', or has the last word already been said? Do we witness, but not say our goodbye to the items mentioned in the poem (l. 1)? In the second stanza, do we take the 'burnt-out candle' to be the subject of 'Shines' (l. 6), 'wasting incense' to be the subject of 'wreathes' (l. 7) and 'hunting-cry' to be the subject of 'Faints' (l. 8), noting that 'the whispering trees of Eden' *must* be the subject of 'Toss on in vain' (l. 11)? Alternatively, do we read 'A hardening darkness' as the subject of all the clauses in the second stanza? In which case we discover how darkness hardens and shines before it wreathes wasting incense to scentless nothing and fainting (making faint) the 'hunting-cry'. Surely de la Mare is creating a structure where all these readings may be plausibly entertained, the rejected interpretation ghosting the chosen one. Moreover, by placing the verb first, the framework of clauses enacts a repeated sense of activity followed by inactivity and dying away, the theme of the poem.

In the version that was nearly included in *The Listeners*, the word in place of 'dismantled' (l. 2) was 'dispetalled', and it may have been dissatisfaction over this that caused de la Mare to hold the poem back from publication. His final choice is a great example of the odd word being the right one, for it plays on the word's literal meaning: '*mantellum*' is the Latin word for cloak, hence 'mantle'; the last flower in the hedge has had her cloak removed. Consciously or unconsciously, Elizabeth Bishop, who called *Come Hither* 'the best anthology I know of', seems to have borrowed de la Mare's use of the word, though not quite its etymological justness, when in her 'Poem' she writes of 'yet-to-be dismantled elms'.[5]

The Railway Junction

From here through tunnelled gloom the track
Forks into two; and one of these
Wheels onward into darkening hills,
And one toward distant seas.

How still it is; the signal light   5
At set of sun shines palely green;
A thrush sings; other sound there's none,
Nor traveller to be seen –

Where late there was a throng. And now,
In peace awhile, I sit alone;   10
Though soon, at the appointed hour,
I shall myself be gone.

But not their way: the bow-legged groom,
The parson in black, the widow and son,
The sailor with his cage, the gaunt   15
Gamekeeper with his gun,

That fair one, too, discreetly veiled –
All, who so mutely came, and went,
Will reach those far nocturnal hills,
Or shores, ere night is spent.   20

I nothing know why thus we met –
Their thoughts, their longings, hopes, their fate:
And what shall I remember, except –
The evening growing late –

That here through tunnelled gloom the track   25
Forks into two; of these
One into darkening hills leads on,
And one toward distant seas?

from *The Fleeting and Other Poems* (1933)

Graham Greene thought the 'dominant symbol' of de la Mare's short stories was the 'railway station or the railway journey'.[1] It's not hard to think of instances to support the contention: his ghost story 'Crewe', for instance. Nor is it difficult to work out why this should be: with their travellers, journeys, waits and departures, their perpetual air of transience, railways and railway stations are the perfect location for some of de la Mare's most characteristic moods and themes.

Railways appear far less often in the verse, but it is hard to imagine a more de la Marean poem than 'The Railway Junction'. Yet it is also a poem that brings to mind other great poems by de la Mare's contemporaries that briefly stop upon a journey: Robert Frost's 'The Road Not Taken' and 'Stopping by Woods on a Snowy Evening' or Edward Thomas's 'Adlestrop', and it is, in a way, conversing with them. For instance, as in reply to how Thomas's poem begins with the affirmation 'Yes. I remember', de la Mare's towards the end asks: 'And what shall I remember, except' (l. 23). Whereas Thomas's singing blackbird has around him 'all the birds/ Of Oxfordshire and Gloucestershire'; de la Mare's thrush is, like himself, quite alone.

As with a wait at a real train station, you can't dwell at 'The Railway Junction' for long without starting to construct narratives for the passengers you see. As is the way with real people-watching, the stories one concocts for the passengers here may proceed from false impressions and assumptions. Is this a groom of horses, 'bow-legged' (l. 13) from riding, or is he a bridegroom? Could the woman in the veil be the groom's bride or does this veil indicate a withdrawal from romantic attachments? Could she even be wearing the veil of a nun? The widow and her son are clearly travelling together, but are they travelling with the parson in black to or from the funeral of her dead husband, or is he travelling to church with the bride and groom? And where are they travelling? The game-keeper and the groom, should he be a groom of horses, will, in the usual way of things, be heading for the hills, and the sailor for the sea, but where the others go is less easy to be sure of.

The poet James Reeves writes that he had read 'The Railway Junction' many times without being sure what it meant, while finding it ever more suggestive. It would be easy, Reeves contends, to read into the poem's situation an 'allegory of human life, but perhaps this would be wrong'.[2] The poem's three routes and seven travellers do have the feel of allegory, and it is possible to construct and then abandon all sorts of allegorical schemes that might fit them. Could 'The Railway Junction' be an allegory of love? If we assume the groom to be a bridegroom, might he not represent roman-tic love? The parson could then represent religious love, the widow the love for the dead or filial love for her son. The sailor could be associated with love of adventure. However, once you start wondering whether the gamekeeper might represent a love of hunting and killing and the woman in the veil a love of mystery, the scheme starts to seem tenuous. Perhaps we should be following another allegorical scheme entirely.

Perhaps we should be looking for a meaning of the poem that is less general and more personal. Do those who were at the railway junction represent stages in de la Mare's own life? 'The evening growing late' (l. 24) appears to be the reason for not remembering, which strongly implies that this evening is also life's evening – de la Mare turned sixty in the year *The Fleeting* was published and, though the evidence is that he continued to have an excellent memory, he may have been aware that he was growing increasingly forgetful. The tunnelled gloom (l. 1) may thus bring to mind the grave, and the 'darkening hills' (l. 3) and 'distant seas' (l. 4) are possibilities for the afterlife. The three routes are also reminiscent of the routes shown in 'Thomas Rymer' (see the notes to 'To K.M.'), in which case de la Mare, as poet, may be *en route* to Elfland, rather than travelling the path of wickedness or the path of righteousness.

As the meanderings above make clear, while there *might* be a single key to this poem, it is hard to find one that opens all its doors. I am more than happy to go along with Reeves's conclusion that all one can be sure of is a 'sense of the loneliness of the human situation', the poem implying that life has a significance that we do not know. As he did in 'The Listeners', in 'The Railway Junction' de la Mare created a poem that encourages us to seek to interpret it again and again, with no real prospect of an all-encompassing answer; it is a poem which feels freighted with a huge, yet never quite defined, emotional significance, and which always seem to elude an attempt to keep its meaning fixed.

To K.M.

And there was a horse in the king's stables:
and the name of the horse was, Genius

We sat and talked . . . It was June, and the summer light
Lay fair upon ceiling and wall as the day took flight.
Tranquil the room – with its colours and shadows wan,
Cherries, and china, and flowers: and the hour slid on.
Dark hair, dark eyes, slim fingers – you made the tea,   5
Pausing with spoon uplifted, to speak to me.
Lulled by our thoughts and our voices, how happy were we!

And, musing, an old, old riddle crept into my head.
'Supposing I just say, *Horse in a field*,' I said,
'What do you *see*?' And we each made answer: 'I –   10
A roan – long tail, and a red-brick house, near by.'
'I – an old cart-horse and rain!' 'Oh no, not rain;
A mare with a long-legged foal by a pond – oh plain!'
'And I, a hedge – and an elm – and the shadowy green
Sloping gently up to the blue, to the west, I mean!' . . .   15

And now: on the field that I see night's darkness lies.
A brook brawls near: there are stars in the empty skies.
The grass is deep, and dense. As I push my way,
From sour-nettled ditch sweeps fragrance of clustering may.
I come to a stile. And lo, on the further side,   20

With still, umbrageous, night-clad fronds, spread wide,
A giant cedar broods. And in crescent's gleam –
A horse, milk-pale, sleek-shouldered, engendered of dream!
Startled, it lifts its muzzle, deep eyes agaze,
Silk-plaited mane . . .   25
                    'Whose pastures are thine to graze?
Creature, delicate, lovely, with woman-like head,
Sphinx-like, gazelle-like? Where tarries thy rider?' I said
And I scanned by that sinking ship's thin twinkling shed
A high-pooped saddle of leather, night-darkened red,   30
Stamped with a pattern of gilding; and over it thrown
A cloak, chain-buckled, with one great glamorous stone,
Wan as the argent moon when o'er fields of wheat
Like Dian she broods, and steals to Endymion's feet.
Interwoven with silver that cloak from seam to seam.   35
And at toss of that head from its damascened bridle did
    beam
Mysterious glare in the dead of the dark . . .
                    'The name,
Fantastical steed? Thy pedigree?
Peace, out of Storm, is the tale? Or *Beauty, of Jeopardy?*   40
The water grieves. Not a footfall – and midnight here.
Why tarries Darkness's bird? Mounded and clear
Slopes to yon hill with its stars the moorland sweet.
There sighs the airs of far heaven. And the dreamer's feet
Scatter the leagues of paths secret to where at last meet   45
Roads called Wickedness, Righteousness, broad-flung or
    strait,

And the third that leads on to the Queen of fair Elfland's
    gate . . .

This then the horse that I see; swift as the wind;
That none may master or mount; and none may bind –
But she, his Mistress: cloaked, and at throat that gem –   50
Dark hair, dark eyes, slim shoulder . . .
        God-speed, K.M.!

        from *The Fleeting and Other Poems* (1933)

Until Kathleen Jones's 2010 book about Katherine Mansfield, 'To K.M.' was assumed to have been conceived as Mansfield's elegy.[1] But, as Jenny McDonnell has since pointed out, the 'origin of the poem is indicative of a mutually supportive working relationship between two *living* writers'.[2] De la Mare published his poem in the *Saturday Westminster Gazette* on 26 January 1922, after first seeking Mansfield's permission.[3] At this point, the poem was called 'Horse in a Field (To Katherine Mansfield)'. Since the typescript of 'Horse in a Field' originally dedicates the poem 'To K.M.', the decision to use her full name may have been made in order to make clear to readers this was the same not-very-well-known writer whose story 'The Garden Party' would be published in the paper the following week.[4] On this occasion, the epigraph was attributed to *The Arabian Nights*. The words of the epigraph do indeed have the ring of Andrew Lang's 1898 translation of the *Nights*, in which the word 'Genius', meaning 'spirit', is used to denote a 'Genie'. However, since the sentence cannot be found there, and since de la Mare subsequently dropped the attribution, I suspect he made it up.

Mansfield used the initials 'K.M.' to sign both her journalism and her letters to de la Mare, but her initials may have had further significance for him. The heroine of de la Mare's 1921 novel *Memoirs of a Midget* goes by the name of Miss M.; de la Mare, writing to Mansfield on 26 May 1921 and anxious that she will enjoy the book, calls Miss M. 'your initialsake, so to speak'.[5] The use of Mansfield's initials may also have been de la Mare's way of placing Mansfield in the same company as 'E.T.'; 'To K.M.' is reminiscent both of the Edward

Thomas tribute '*Sotto Voce*' and 'To Thomas Hardy', and is placed next to '*Sotto Voce*' in the 1942 edition of his *Collected Poems*. The poem is written in an iambic pentameter, but one which employs a huge amount of metrical variation, which allows de la Mare to replicate some of the incantatory effects of his lyric metres, particularly in the poem's second half. (He breaks away from the metre in ll. 37–9 and ll. 51–2).

'To K.M.' begins by recalling an encounter between de la Mare and Mansfield which took place in her Hampstead house in June 1920 and a moment of lulled reverie and daydream, shared 'as the day took flight' (l. 2).[6] Mansfield likewise associated her bond with de la Mare with a room's fading light. In her journal entry of 1 January 1922, when she was writing her story 'The Doves' Nest', Mansfield records: 'Read W.J.D.'s [i.e. de la Mare's] poems. I feel very near to him in mind. I want to remember how the light fades from a room – and one fades with it, is expunged, sitting still, knees together, hands in pockets . . .'[7]

The description of the room as 'tranquil' (l. 3), like the use of the word 'genius', recalls de la Mare's review of Mansfield's first mature short story collection *Bliss* in *The Athenaeum* of 21 January 1921 (Mansfield had asked her husband J. Middleton Murry, the magazine's editor, for de la Mare to be offered the book for review):[8]

[T]he pitch of mind is invariably emotional, the poise lyrical. None the less that mind is absolutely tranquil and attentive in its intellectual grasp of the matter in hand. And though all, Miss Mansfield's personality, whatever its disguises, haunts her work just as its customary inmate may haunt a vacant room, its *genius* a place.[9]

Mansfield's companion Ida Baker, who was making conversation with the other de la Mares present that teatime, records 'Katherine's queer little habit of holding her spoon in the air after stirring the cup. She was in the middle of a sentence, probably, and could not remember to put it down.'[10] As an old man, de la Mare would say to Theresa Whistler, 'You had only to see the way she held a spoon . . . to see how wonderful she was.'[11]

The lulling of 'thoughts and our voices' (l. 7) is a prelude to enchantment: de la Mare is 'musing' (l. 8) – pondering, daydreaming and treating Mansfield as a muse – when an 'old, old riddle' (l. 8) creeps into his head, probably because of that riddle's similarity both to Mansfield's pen name and her maiden name, which was Beauchamp ('beautiful field'). Like the riddle of the Sphinx (l. 28) (What creature walks on four legs in the morning, two legs at noon and three legs in the afternoon? Answer: man), the riddle of the horse in a field is to be answered by seeing oneself in what it figures. In their correspondence, de la Mare and Mansfield both recall how Mansfield had seen a small chestnut horse; nevertheless, the poem has her see a roan, a switch made for reasons of symbolism.[12] Half of the hairs on a roan are white: it is thus a subdued, daylight version of the white horse that will appear later in the poem. An old carthorse and rain suggest that de la Mare is feeling his years; if Mansfield sees a mare and a foal, her mind may be turning towards motherhood. The view of the West with the last teatime horse in a field evokes life's evening for de la Mare, the 'blue' the void or perhaps heaven, the West the place of the setting of the sun.

The 'And now' of line 16 indicates a momentous change (probably de la Mare's reading of *Bliss*). In place of the flowers of teatime we have nettles and 'clustering may' (l. 19), the flower of the hawthorn (see notes to '"The Hawthorn Hath a Deathly Smell"') that is a portal to the Other World of Fairie, as it is in 'The Fairies' by William Allingham (1824–89), and the cedar, the tree traditionally associated with immortality.[13]

Though the 'horse, milk-pale' (l. 23) might easily be mistaken for the pale horse of Death to be found in Revelation 6:8, it is that of the Queen of Elfland, as depicted in the medieval border ballad 'Thomas Rymer'.[14] According to the version of the ballad collected by de la Mare in *Come Hither*, True Thomas 'lay oer yond grassy bank' and beholds a 'lady gay' riding a 'milk-white steed' from whose mane hangs fifty-nine silver bells.[15] She was 'brisk and bold' and has a mantle of fine velvet and a 'grass-green skirt'. Thomas takes off his hat and hails her as the Queen of Heaven. She corrects him, saying that she is 'but the queen of fair Elfland' come to visit him and that he must serve her for seven years. She takes Thomas behind her on her horse and, following the adventures of forty days and forty nights, shows him the narrow road of righteousness, the broad road of wickedness and 'that bonny road which winds about the ferny brae' (steep hillside or bank) 'That is the road to fair Elfland' where the two of them must go (hence ll. 46–7).[16] Thomas, now suitably attired in a coat 'of the even cloth' and a pair of velvet green shoes, is not seen on earth for seven years.

It is clear from de la Mare's note to 'Thomas Rymer' in *Come Hither* that he is familiar with different versions of the text. He also informs the reader that Thomas meets his Queen while day-dreaming under the Eildon Tree, which is by tradition a hawthorn.[17] De la Mare would also have been aware that the thirteenth-century figure Thomas the Rhymer, otherwise known as True Thomas or Thomas of Ercledoune, had a reputation not just as a poet, but also as a seer, his gift having been bestowed upon this journey.

Mansfield the friend at teatime and Mansfield the muse have disappeared, to be replaced by the horse in the field that is her revealed genius. The moon is a 'sinking ship' (l. 29); the saddle is 'high-pooped' (a poop being the cabin at the rear of a ship). The nautical imagery may obliquely recall Mansfield's having originally sailed from New Zealand, or more likely how, when the poem was written, she was living in France and attempting to recover from tuberculosis. *Bliss*, and this vision, would have journeyed 'riderless' to de la Mare over the sea. But the description is also anticipating the 'God-speed K.M.' (l. 52) that wishes Mansfield well on her great journey. Though this is a dream vision rather than a literal description, Mansfield did possess a magnificent 'cloak, chain-buckled' (l. 32) with a damask lining. 'Like Dian she broods, and steals to Endymion's feet' (l. 34) refers to the myth of Endymion. In the Roman version of the Greek myth, Diana, goddess of the moon but also of chastity, fell in love with Endymion, visiting him in his sleep, a story which has an obvious appropriateness to this dream vision. De la Mare would have known the story from Keats's *Endymion* and may also be thinking of the tale as an allegory of Platonic love, as it is in the painting *Diana and Endymion* by Francesco Solimena (1657–1747). The horse is male, so presumably it is analogous to the female muses and other anima-like figures that de la Mare uses to represent his own creative spirit (see the notes to 'Reflections' and 'Sallie'). While it is beautiful and intricately apparelled, it is idealised rather than sanitised: Mansfield and her genius are to take a road beyond Wickedness or Righteousness. The horse's pedigree suggests its peace and beauty are the products of jeopardy and storm (l. 40).

That June teatime was the last meeting of Mansfield and de la Mare, but it was important for both writers. 'I love Delamare [sic], love the man who came to tea – with his wife sitting there by the fire and dark, young, lovely Florence. The memory of that afternoon is so precious,' wrote Katherine Mansfield to John Middleton Murry in a letter of 12 October 1920.[18] Mansfield now viewed de la Mare as an ideal reader ('*This* one I'd like you and de la Mare to like – other people don't matter,' she writes to Murry, sending him her story 'The Lady's Maid' in December 1920). She repeatedly wondered what to give de la Mare in her will. Her treasured ivory mirror? Her much-loved copy of Shakespeare? Another of her books? But it was to be her posthumous collection *The Doves' Nest* which, being dedicated 'To Walter de la Mare', returned the gift made by 'To K.M.'.

'Horse in a Field' was to appear again in what was now the *Weekly Westminster Gazette* on 20 January 1923 alongside

Mansfield's obituary, where it acted as an elegy.[19] The poem was collected under the present title, without the epigraph, in the American volume *The Captive and Other Poems* (1928) and in the British volume *The Fleeting* (1933), with the epigraph but without the attribution to *The Arabian Nights*.

In the revised edition of *Come Hither*, de la Mare's note to Robert Herrick's 'Upon a Child That Died' reflects on dying young or old, concluding with the words: 'And in those who have not become old but who are soon to die the radiance of this new light is sometimes seen to shine. As if by a secret forewarning they have made haste in mind and spirit far beyond their years – Keats, Emily Brontë, Katherine Mansfield.'[20]

The Feckless Dinner-Party

'Who are we waiting for?' '*Soup* burnt?' '. . . Eight–'
   'Only the tiniest party. – Us!'
'Darling! Divine!' 'Ten minutes late –'
   'And my digest –' 'I'm *rav*enous!'
'"Toomes"?' – 'Oh, he's new.' 'Looks crazed, I guess.'   5
   '"Married" – *Again*!' 'Well; more or less!'

'Dinner is *served*!' '"Dinner is served"!'
   'Is served?' 'Is served.' 'Ah, yes.'

'Dear Mr. Prout, will you take down
   The Lilith in leaf-green by the fire?   10
Blanche Ogleton? . . .' 'How coy a frown! –
   Hasn't she borrowed *Eve*'s attire?'
'Morose Old Adam!' 'Charmed – I vow.'
   'Come then, and meet her now.'

'Now, Dr. Mallus – would you please? –   15
   Our daring poetess, Delia Seek?'
'The lady with the bony knees?'
   'And – *entre nous* – less song than beak.'
'Sharing her past with Simple Si –'
   '*Bare* facts! He'll blush!' 'Oh, fie!'   20

'And *you*, Sir Nathan – false but fair! –
   That fountain of wit, Aurora Pert.'
'More wit than It, poor dear! But there . . .'
   'Pitiless Pacha! *And* such a flirt!'
'"Flirt"! *Me*?' 'Who else?' 'You here . . . Who can . . . ?'   25
   'In*corr*igible man!'

'And now, Mr. Simon – little me! –
   Last and –' 'By no means least!' 'Oh, come!
What naughty, naughty flattery!
   Honey! – I *hear* the creatures hum!'   30
'Sweets for the sweet, *I* always say!'
   '"Always"? . . . We're last.' '*This* way?' . . .

'No, sir; straight on, please.' 'I'd have vowed! –
   I came the other . . .' 'It's queer; I'm sure . . .'
'What frightful pictures!' 'Fiends!' 'The *crowd!*'   35
   'Such nudes!' 'I can't endure . . .'

'Yes, *there* they go.' 'Heavens! *Are* we right?'
   'Follow up closer!' '"Prout"? – sand-blind!'
'This endless . . .' 'Who's turned down the light?'
   'Keep calm! They're close behind.'   40

'Oh! Dr. Mallus; what dismal stairs!'
   'I hate these old Victor . . .' 'Dry rot!'
'Darker and darker!' 'Fog!' 'The air's . . .'
   'Scarce breathable!' 'Hell!' '*What*?'

'The banister's gone!' 'It's deep; keep close!'   45
   'We're going down and down!' 'What fun!'
'Damp! Why, my shoes . . .' 'It's slimy . . . Not *moss!*'
   'I'm freezing cold!' 'Let's run.'

'. . . Behind us. I'm giddy . . .' 'The catacombs . . .'
   'That shout!' 'Who's there?' 'I'm *alone!*' 'Stand back!'   50
'She said, Lead . . .' 'Oh!' 'Where's Toomes?' '*Toomes!*'
   'TOOMES!'
   'Stifling!' 'My skull will crack!'

'Sir Nathan! *Ai!*' 'I *say*! *Toomes!* Prout!'
   'Where? Where?' '"Our silks and fine array" . . .'   55
'She's mad.' 'I'm dying!' 'Oh, Let me *out!*'
   'My God! We've lost our way!' . . .

And now how sad-serene the abandoned house,
Whereon at dawn the spring-tide sunbeams beat;
And time's slow pace alone is ominous,   60
And naught but shadows of noonday therein meet;
Domestic microcosm, only a Trump could rouse:
And, pondering darkly, in the silent rooms,
He who misled them all – the butler, Toomes.

from *The Fleeting and Other Poems* (1933)

'The Feckless Dinner-Party' is, with the exception of the last stanza, conveyed in direct speech: snippets of conversation from oh-so-sophisticated society guests on their way to a delayed meal. Their journey proves an unexpectedly long one; carnal gossip gives way to observations about what it's like downstairs: the 'frightful pictures' of 'nudes' (ll. 35–6), the bad air (l. 43), the darkness, something slimy, which may well be considerably nastier than moss (l. 47). 'Hell!' (l. 44) says one of the would-be diners, without intended irony, but that is their likely destination. The butler Toomes has led them astray, and only he is left behind.

It would be natural to interpret the reference to 'Eight' in the first line as indicating the time dinner was supposed to be served. However, since the next speaker takes 'Eight' as referring to those at the dinner party, it must refer to the number of the diners (an early version of the poem begins: 'Every one here?' 'Yes;-six-seven-eight').[1] If that's the case, there might appear to have been a miscount. Toomes, as butler, presumably isn't included among 'Us' (l. 2); 'The Lilith in leaf-green by the fire' (l. 10) sounds like a description of Blanche Ogleton and not of a separate guest. But that would leave us with seven: Ogleton, Dr Mallus, Delia Seek, Mr Simon, Sir Nathan, Aurora Pert and Mr Prout (an old spelling of 'proud' and, like Ogleton and Mallus, a clearly Dickensian surname). Assuming the usual dinner party arrangement of an equal number of men and women, we are one female guest short.

But perhaps we have been too quick to count. The diner asking Mr Prout to take down 'The Lilith in leaf-green by the fire' (l. 10) is unsure whether she is Blanche Ogleton or not; in response, she coyly frowns. So Blanche Ogleton may be another of the party and Lilith the missing eighth guest. Lilith is more or less absent from the Bible, but she was, according to Jewish tradition, Adam's first wife who refused to lie down beneath him and be subservient to him. She is a female demon who also figures in a number of ancient Middle Eastern mythologies and, when not blamed for the death of young children, is a byword for unrestrained female sexuality. Closer to de la Mare's own time and culture, Lilith is depicted in well-known nineteenth-century paintings, such as *Lady Lilith* by Dante Gabriel Rossetti and the near-pornographic *Lilith with a Snake* by John Collier. She is also present in D. G. Rossetti's poem 'Eden Bower' and is the subject of George MacDonald's 1895 prose romance *Lilith*. In the early twentieth century, the name had enough currency for the reference to 'The Lilith in leaf-green' to be taken as a highbrow joke about a vampy-looking woman whose skimpy green costume reminds the speaker of a fig-leafed Eve after the fall. Mr Prout responds by chafing the speaker about the 'Old Adam' (l. 13), meaning man's inherently sinful nature, but also perhaps the fact that the lady in question was once his lover. However, since this is a poem in which 'Hell!' turns out to be literal, there is a possibility that this Lilith has been the wife of the literal Adam. If so, '"Married" – *Again*!' 'Well; more or less!' (l. 6) gives us a clue as to the possible identity of Toomes. In MacDonald's *Lilith*, she is married to 'The Shadow', while in earlier versions of the story, her more-or-less husband is Samael, the Angel of Death (de la Mare was familiar with the figure of Samael and mentions him in *Come Hither*).[2]

'The Feckless Dinner-Party' is a fireworks display from a poet not usually inclined to be showy. Among the devices employed to capture the voices are sharply used italics and inverted commas: for instance, the incredulous italics of '*Soup* burnt?' (l. 1) or the inverted commas around '"Married"' (l. 6) which manage at once to indicate both the way the word has been picked up from another conversation and the sort of marriage involved. The poem also displays a very acute ear for rising and falling of pitches of conversation and how these may be enhanced by metre. In his unpublished essay 'Meaning in Poetry', de la Mare remarks:

> A versifier must convey all such inflexions and intonation in his verse, in spite, as it were, of his imposed metre. He must, as far as possible, ensure that his context shall reveal the emphases, the rhythms, the tune of what he is saying.
>
> Take, for example, merely so distinctly matter-of-fact a statement as 'It's no use asking her to change her mind.' At first glance we might not recognise this as verse at all. Yet verse it certainly may be. 'It's no use asking her to change her mind' – an iambic pentameter. By varying its context and therefore its rhythm we can, as it were, escape from its metre and so reveal and emphasise differing shades and degrees of meaning.[3]

De la Mare then gives examples of how this may be done. 'The Feckless Dinner-Party' performs similar metrical feats with a well-disguised ballad metre of four and sometimes three stresses (the narratorial voice of the last verse is in iambic pentameter).

Since 'The Feckless Dinner-Party' appeared in a collection of 1933, it might appear to be the beneficiary of two influential works: T. S. Eliot's modernist long poem *The Waste Land* (1922), which introduced the public to the poetry of unattributed direct speech by multiple speakers, and *The Door*, Mary Roberts Rinehart's murder mystery of 1930, which popularised the idea that 'the butler did it'. However, an earlier version of de la Mare's poem, entitled 'The Dinner Party', appears in the original typescript for 1921's *The Veil*, so neither can have been a formative influence (the modernist who probably *did* influence the poem was Katherine Mansfield). Indeed, had de la Mare published the poem in 1921, he might now be seen as something of a trailblazer for the modernist poets, particularly since 'The Dinner-Party' lacks that unmodernist last stanza of the finished poem. But while modernists and stylistic purists are welcome to place the lines after 'My God! We've lost our way!' (l. 57) under a rectangle of paper, others may well be grateful for that last verse. Not only does it have the good manners to explain to any readers who are lost what on earth has been going on; after all the hubbub, it has an Alka-Seltzer calm.

The 1921 date for the poem also means that the original inspiration for the poem cannot have been, as Richard Davenport-Hines suggests, the society dinner parties of Lady Desborough which the de la Mares were obliged to attend when they moved to a house by Taplow Court in 1925 and gained Lord Desborough as a landlord.[4] There were, however, other dinner parties attended by de la Mare in the years up to 1921 which might have given him the idea for the poem (for someone who would happily consign some dinner party-goers to the infernal pit, de la Mare had a moth-like propensity to hang around their flames). While the characters here are presumably meant to be types rather than identifiable people, 'Our daring poetess, Delia Seek' (l. 16) bears a striking similarity to the memorably large-beaked and 'daring' aristocratic modernist, Edith Sitwell.

l. 24, 'pacha' a variant spelling of 'pasha', a high-ranking Turkish official, the title is here used figuratively.

l. 54, 'Our silks and fine array' alludes to William Blake's song 'My silks and fine array'.

l. 62, 'only a Trump could rouse' alludes to the trumpet at the biblical day of judgement, Corinthians 1, 15: 52.

Reflections

Three Sisters – and the youngest
   Was yet lovelier to see
Than wild flower palely blooming
   Under Ygdrasil Tree,

Than this well at the woodside   5
   Whose waters silver show,
Though in womb of the blind earth
   Ink-like, ebon, they flow.

Creeps on the belled bindweed;
   The bee, in hoverings nigh,   10
Sucks his riches of nectar;
   Clouds float in the sky;

And she, O pure vanity,
   Newly-wakened, at that brink,
Crouches close, smiling dreamlike,   15
   To gaze, not to drink.

She sees not earth's morning
   Darkly framed in that cold deep:
Naught, naught but her beauty
   Made yet fairer by sleep.   20

And though glassed in that still flood
   She peer long, and long,
As faithful stays that image,
   As echo is to song . . .

Anon – in high noontide   25
   Comes her sister, wan with fear,
Lest the love in her bosom
   Even the bright birds should hear

Wail divine grieved enchantment.
   She kneels; and, musing, sighs;   30
Unendurable strangenesses
   Darken the eyes

That meet her swift searchings.
   From her breast there falls a flower.
Down, down – as she ponders –   35
   The fair petals shower,

Hiding brow, mouth, cheek – all
   That reflected there is seen.
And she gone, that Mirror
   As of old rests serene . . .   40

Comes moth-light, faint dusk-shine,
   The green woods still and whist;
And their sister, the eldest
   To keep her late tryst.

Long thought and lone broodings 45
    Have wanned, have withered, lined
A face, without beauty,
    Which no dream hath resigned

To love's impassioned grieving.
    She stands. The louring air 50
Breathes cold on her cheekbone,
    Stirs thief-like her hair;

And a still quiet challenge
    Fills her dark, her flint-grey eyes,
As she lifts her bowed head 55
    To survey the cold skies.

Wherein stars, hard and restless,
    Burn in station fore-ordained,
As if mocking for ever
    A courage disdained. 60

And she stoops wearied shoulders,
    Void of scorn, of fear, or ruth,
To confront in that well-spring
    The dark gaze of Truth.

from *The Fleeting and Other Poems* (1933)

Ygdrasil (l. 4) is the great ash tree of Norse mythology, whose limbs represent the universe. Beneath it lies Urth's Well, to which each day come three maidens, the three Norns, and set in it men's fates. The three sisters of 'Reflections' appear to be, if not the Norns themselves, at least their first cousins. The first is like Urd, the Norn who represents the past; the second is like Verdandi, who represents the present, and the third is akin to Skuld, who represents the future. De la Mare may also be thinking of other equivalent myths: given the grey eyes (l. 54) he may have in mind the Graeae, or 'Grey Ones', the Roman fates; he may also be thinking of the Three Graces.

In 'Reflections', the first sister is come straight from slumber. '[L]ovelier' than the natural world about her, the wild flower and the well, she is 'dreamlike' (l. 15) with 'beauty' (l. 19) made 'yet fairer by sleep' (l. 20): vain, perhaps narcissistic, yet 'faithful' (l. 23) to her own beauty's image. The second is full of fearful secret love, 'divine grieved enchantment' (l. 29); at first, she sees her eyes darkened in the well by 'unendurable strangeness' (l. 31), until the flower petals fallen from her breast obscure her face. The third has been 'wanned' and 'withered' by 'Long thought' and 'lone broodings' (ll. 45–6), without beauty and dreams of love. Weary she may be, but it is she who confronts the 'dark gaze of Truth' (l. 64).

Given the fact that each sister is differently concerned with her own reflection, this must in part be a poem about self-perception; and given the sisters' different ages, it is a poem that refers to stages of one's life. There is a strong hint that we may read this as a poem of 'reflections' on writing – however silver they may look in the well, the waters flow 'Ink-like' (l. 8) in the womb of the earth – or at least the imagination. For those who want to consider 'Reflections' as an allegory of the imagination, the ideas in de la Mare's essay 'Rupert Brooke and the Intellectual Imagination' serve as useful background information.[1] The essay makes a distinction between the idealised Child and the Boy (de la Mare admits that he isn't sure as to how far his idealised Boy applies to girls). Children, says de la Mare, make no great distinction between dreams and actuality and are contemplatives, solitaries and visionaries. As the nursery gives way to the school proper (a transition that would have been two or three years later for a child of de la Mare's time and class than it is for most children now), the Child becomes the Boy and a curious investigator of the facts and thoughts of the outside world. Likewise, the

poetical imagination [. . .] is of two distinct kinds or type: the one divines, while the other discovers. The one is intuitive, inductive; the other logical, deductive. The one is visionary, the other intellectual. The one knows beauty is truth, the other reveals that truth is beauty. And the poet inherits . . . the one kind from the child in him, the other from the boy in him. Not that any one poet's imagination is purely and solely of either type. The greatest poets – Shakespeare, Dante, Goethe, for instance, are masters of both. There is a borderland in which dwell Wordsworth, Keats, [Coventry] Patmore, Mr T. S. Eliot and many others.[2]

But examples of the visionaries and dreamers, 'those whose

eyes are set inward': 'Plato, Plotinus, the writer of the book of Job, Blake, Vaughan [. . .] W. B. Yeats' – may be taken as representative of one type and 'Lucretius, Dryden, Pope, Byron, Meredith and Alice Meynell' as representatives of the other. The imagination of de la Mare himself, we may gather, is, unlike that of Rupert Brooke, much less that of a boy than it is that of a child.

De la Mare could be dismissive of Sigmund Freud and what de la Mare reckoned to be his over-emphasis on sex. Nevertheless, 'Reflections' does strongly bring to mind Freud's 'The Theme of the Three Caskets', an essay in which he reflects on Shakespeare's *The Merchant of Venice* and how it is not the gold nor the silver but the lead casket that Portia's suitor must choose if he is to win her, and relates this to a scene in *King Lear*, where it is not the flattering Goneril and Regan but the third daughter, the near-silent Cordelia, who is the worthy one. This is a structure that is also found in folk tales. For instance, the put-upon Cinderella is the worthy third daughter but hides herself. In these examples and in other folk tales, Freud traces this virtuous dumbness of the third daughter and third suitor, going on to identify the third's dumbness with that of death and averring that stories which emphasise the virtue or marriageability of the third daughter conceal this darker identification. Freud then points out that 'if the third of the sisters is the Goddess of Death, the sisters are known to us. They are the Fates, the Moerae, the Parcae or the Norns, the third of whom is called Atropos, the inexorable.'[3] Whether or not de la Mare knew this essay, he certainly knew Freud's source tales intimately.

Rose

Three centuries now are gone
    Since Thomas Campion
Left men his airs, his verse, his heedful prose.
    Few other memories
    Have we of him, or his,   5
And, of his sister, none, but that her name was Rose.

    Woodruff, far moschatel
    May the more fragrant smell
When into brittle dust their blossoming goes.
    His, too, a garden sweet,   10
    Where rarest beauties meet,
And, as a child, he shared them with this Rose.

    Faded, past changing, now,
    Cheek, mouth, and childish brow.
Where, too, her phantom wanders no man knows.   15
    Yet, when in undertone
    That eager lute pines on,
Pleading of things he loves, it sings of Rose.

from *The Fleeting and Other Poems* (1933)

'A rose by any other name would smell as sweet,' says Juliet to Romeo. Still, Juliet's view discounts the magic of the particular sound of the word: its similarity to 'arose', for instance, and all the many connotations that the word may bring, including ones quite particular to the listener. What if your own sister happened to be called Rose? Wouldn't just a little of her cling to its every use? And what would that say about a poet who was fond of putting roses in his poems?

De la Mare felt a special admiration for the Elizabethan lyric poet Thomas Campion. In 1910, he wrote: 'No other poems in the language have quite their bird-like exquisite movement. They vibrate with a frail delicate music that sings, dies away and reawakes, like the voice of a bird in the shadowy moonlight of a wood.'[1] As W. H. Auden noticed, de la Mare's own delicate music – and 'Rose' is a beautifully turned example of it – has learned much from Campion's.[2] De la Mare's note to Thomas Campion's 'There Is a Garden in Her Face' in *Come Hither* reads:

Thomas Campion was 'borne upon Ash Weddensday being the twelfth day of February. An. Rg. Eliz. nono' – 1567. He had one sister, Rose. He was educated at Peterhouse, Cambridge, and this was his yearly allowance of clothes: 'A gowne, a cap, a hat, ii dublets, ii payres of hose, iiii payres of netherstockes, vi payre of shoes, ii shirts, and two bandes.' He was allowed also one quire of paper every quarter; and a half a pound of candles every fortnight from Michaelmas to Lady Day. He studied law, may for a time have fought as a soldier in France, and became a physician. He died on March 1, 1620, and was buried the same day at St. Dunstan's in the West, Fleet Street, the entry in the register under that date being 'Thomas Campion, doctor of Phisicke, was buried.'

I have taken these particulars from Mr S. P. Vivian's edition of his poems, because it is pleasant to share even this of the little that is known of a man who was not only a fine and original poet and 'a most curious metrist' – though for two centuries a forgotten one – but also because he was one of the chief songwriters in the great age of English Music. Like all good craftsmen, he endeavoured to do his work 'well, surely, cleanly, workmanly, substantially, curiously, and sufficiently,' as did the glaziers of King's College Chapel, which is distant but a kingfisher's flight over a strip of lovely water from his own serene Peterhouse. It seems a little curious that being himself a lover of music he should have at first detested rhyming in verse. But he lived none the less to write such delicate rhymed poems as this.

In the preface to his *Book of Ayres*, he says, 'I have chiefly aymed to couple my Words and Notes *lovingly* together, which will be much for him to doe that hath not power over both.'[3]

De la Mare's own much-loved younger sister also had a flower name: she was known as 'Poppy'.

l. 3. 'heedful': John Bayley refers to this, with its 'slight air of gentle mocking mystery' as 'the *mot juste*, but what an evasive and puckish *mot juste* it is'.[4]

l. 7. 'Woodruff': a sweet-scented white flower with four petals, which flowers in the early spring; 'moschatel' is a small green flower known for its musky smell, which flowers in early May; it grows in a great number of countries and climates, thus qualifying for the epithet 'far'. Both flowers appear to be mentioned for their smell and especially for their enhanced fragrance after they have been wilted or dried (as in potpourri), this being a sort of lingering after death. The rose that is Campion's sister lingers as a sort of faint scent in her brother's poems, never exactly mentioned, but often named.

Away

There is no sorrow
Time heals never;
No loss, betrayal,
Beyond repair.
Balm for the soul, then,   5
Though grave shall sever
Lover from loved
And all they share;
See, the sweet sun shines,
The shower is over,   10
Flowers preen their beauty,
The day how fair!
Brood not too closely
On love, or duty;
Friends long forgotten   15
May wait you where
Life with death
Brings all to an issue;
None will long mourn for you,
Pray for you, miss you,   20
Your place left vacant,
You not there.

from *Memory and Other Poems* (1938)

Commentaries such as these have a habit of prizing those poems they can say most about. The beautifully turned poem that says exactly what needs to be said in the clearest terms can make commentary seem redundant, but the danger is that the excellence of such poems then passes unremarked. Moreover, 'Away' is in other ways not a poem which draws attention to itself.

That might be one of the lessons to take from its appearance in the short story 'Face' by Alice Munro (other possible significances are discussed by Angela Leighton in her book *Hearing Things*).[1] In the story, the words 'None will long mourn for you,/ Pray for you, miss you,/ Your place vacant' are read to the narrator, probably in a dream, by a 'girl-child phantom' as he lies temporarily blinded and in hospital.[2] The narrator, who has recited many poems in his work as an actor for radio, has guessed the authors of all the other poems she has read out apart from this one. Later he finds the poem and the name of its author written on a piece of paper concealed in a book he had intended to give to a charity bazaar; it may well have been written out by a girl he knew in childhood who was sympathetic to his disfiguring birthmark. Suitably for a story about de la Mare, she seems to be at once the narrator's double and also his anima (see the notes to 'Autumn' and 'Sallie').

What's interesting about the story, and indeed the poem, is that the narrator takes comfort in the poem's words, and yet these words are in some ways very bleak. You will die and soon enough be forgotten. Yes, time heals, but it takes away more or less everything as it does so. A school of critical opinion, beginning with de la Mare's old adversary F. R. Leavis, still takes it as an article of faith that a poem which consoles the reader must somehow be at fault, must be pulling the wool over our eyes. But 'Away' and poems like it prove there *are* consoling poems that look the bleak and inevitable firmly in the face. It is possible that the poet regards death with such equanimity because he is confident of an afterlife, yet while lines 15–18 don't deny one, they don't clearly affirm it either and may simply refer to memories at the moment of death.

'Away', like 'Fare Well', is a poem which shows a rare generosity in the face of mortality: the thought that you won't be long mourned should please you, if you think more of the happiness of your loved ones than the need for everyone to ache at your absence. While the poem has little in the way of imagery to show its gratitude for life's wonder, there is a marvellous image of flowers preening their beauty in line 11, like birds doing the same following a rain shower. The short lines, with their variation between two and, occasionally, three stresses, are beautifully handled. Every bit as impressive is the irregular rhyme scheme: 'never' (l. 2), 'sever' (l. 6) and 'over' (l. 10); 'beauty' (l. 11) and 'duty' (l. 14) ('closely' (l. 13) may be counted as a near-rhyme); 'issue' (l. 18) and 'miss you' (l. 20) ('for you' (l. 19) looks more like a rhyme than it is – the 'oo' sound in the other words is unstressed), and, stretching across nearly the entire poem, 'repair' (l. 4), 'share' (l. 8), 'fair' (l. 12), 'where' (l. 16) and 'there (l. 22).

Thomas Hardy

Mingled the moonlight with daylight – the last in the
  narrowing west;
Silence of nightfall lay over the shallowing valleys at rest
      In the Earth's green breast:
Yet a small multitudinous singing, a lully of voices of birds,
Unseen in the vague shelving hollows, welled up with my
  questioning words: 5
All Dorsetshire's larks for connivance of sweetness seemed
  trysting to greet
Him in whose songs the bodings of raven and nightingale meet.

Stooping and smiling, he questioned, 'No birdnotes myself
  do I hear?
Perhaps 'twas the talk of chance farers, abroad in the hush
  with us here –
      In the dusk-light clear?'   10
And there peered from his eyes, as I listened, a concourse of
  women and men,
Whom his words had made living, long-suffering – they
  flocked to remembrance again;
'O Master,' I cried in my heart, 'lorn thy tidings, grievous
  thy song;
Yet thine, too, this solacing music, as we earthfolk stumble
  along.'

from *Memory and Other Poems* (1933)

While clearing out a cupboard in 1918, Thomas Hardy chanced upon a hugely enthusiastic 1910 review of his gigantic dramatic poem for the page, *The Dynasts*. The name of the reviewer, Walter de la Mare, which had meant next to nothing to Hardy in 1910, now conveyed to him 'those delightful sensations of moonlight & forests & haunted houses which I myself seem to have visited'.[1] Hardy wrote to de la Mare to begin a friendship which would last until his death.

On 16 June 1921, de la Mare came to stay with him at his house in Max Gate. De la Mare would recall in a radio broadcast of 1955:

> We actually met on Dorchester Station's down platform. He showed a child's satisfaction and a rare courtesy almost peculiar to himself, in his immediate apology that in spite of every effort he had failed to get me a cab simply because the complete fleet of Dorchester's cabs had been secured by people with tickets for the first performance of a dramatised version of *Tess* [Theresa Whistler points out it was, in fact, *The Mellstock Quire* that the Hardy Players performed that week[2]]. Therefore, having compelled me to give my bag into his keeping, we set out on foot. And soon, as it seemed, our footsteps were muffled by the beautiful moss-quiet turf of his Dorsetshire downs.
>
> Suddenly, in the midst of our talk, under the immense canopy of the pale-blue latening sky, not far from the sea of course, I became aware of a captivating, low, trilling chorus of birds, coming as it seemed from a shallow hollow of the downs no more than some thirty paces

distant. I put up a finger and enquired of him what birds they were. We came to a standstill, he eyed me with a characteristically tilted glance that was never penetrating – always divining and comprehending – and replied that he could hear no birds. We continued after a few moments on our way. Were the birds that I had heard then really nature's; or had Hardy magicked them into my mind?[3]

The next day, the two poets, along with Hardy's second wife Florence, went to Stinsford churchyard. The Hardy family graves were underneath a yew, and Hardy had brought along a small spade-like implement in order to scrape off the moss. De la Mare said he preferred his tombstones green.[4] The visit prompted Hardy to seek de la Mare's advice on his poem 'Voices From Things Growing in a Country Graveyard'.[5] After encouraging Hardy to finish the poem and offering some suggestions, de la Mare then placed it in the *London Mercury* for Hardy.[6] The poem was presumably shown to de la Mare on account of his interest in ghosts, epitaphs and graveyards. Whether or not on account of de la Mare's influence or suggestion, 'Voices From Things Growing in a Country Graveyard' has lines that sound like the many imaginary epitaphs de la Mare had already written, both as standalone poems and in the graveyard stories eventually collected in *Ding Dong Bell* (1924). The description of the little girl 'poor Fanny Hurd', whose voice from the grave declares that she once fluttered 'like a bird/ Above the grass, as now I wave/ In daisy shapes above my grave', in particular, sounds more like de la Mare than Hardy. While it isn't always easy to tell where

mutual preoccupations end and influence begins, there is bet-
ween the work of the two writers a fascinating connecting
web, one which is currently being examined by Yui Kajita.[7]

Though published in *Memory* (1938), an earlier version of
'Thomas Hardy' entitled 'To Thomas Hardy' was intended
for *The Fleeting*, only to be omitted at proof stage, and the
title indicates that the first draft of the poem was written while
Hardy was still alive. Similarities to '*Sotto Voce*' and 'To K.M.'
are clearly deliberate: the poems were conceived close to one
another and form a triptych celebrating three writer friends
for whom de la Mare felt affinity and admiration. '*Sotto Voce*'
and 'To K.M.' are written in a style that is thoroughly de la
Mare's own, while 'Thomas Hardy' is more of an *hommage*: a
sonnet written in a manner that is deliberately close to Hardy's.
The word 'Master' (l. 13) is not mere flattery; de la Mare
regarded Hardy as the greatest writer of his lifetime.

This is a 'lully' (l. 4) of birds and not a 'lullay', so we are
presumably not supposed to think of John Skelton's use of
the word, as we are in '*Sotto Voce*', but of the more straight-
forward lulling that may be prelude to vision, the sort we have
in 'To K.M.'. 'All Dorsetshire's larks' (l. 6) echoes Thomas's
'Adlestrop', which listens to 'all the birds/ Of Oxfordshire
and Gloucestershire'; it is the sound of the natural world.[8]
Hardy does not hear this sound. Still, listening to birds is a
way of hearing his genius. By writing of a mixing of nightin-
gale and raven in Hardy's 'songs' (l. 7), de la Mare may not
just be referring to the less melodious aspects of Hardy's verse
but also to the fact that the raven is both a bird of ill omen and
a noted mimic of the human voice – a novelist among birds. It

is, for once, not hearing that gives de la Mare his moment of insight, but looking into Hardy's eyes where appear the 'concourse of women and men' (l. 11) from his works flocking like birds. If Hardy's tidings are '[for]lorn' (l. 13), in that they are full of disturbing post-Christian pessimism, it was a pessimism which de la Mare sometimes shared.

Dry August Burned

Dry August burned. A harvest hare
Limp on the kitchen table lay,
Its fur blood-blubbered, eye astare,
While a small child that stood near by
Wept out her heart to see it there.   5

Sharp came the *clop* of hoofs, the clang
Of dangling chain, voices that rang.
Out like a leveret she ran,
To feast her glistening bird-clear eyes
On a team of field artillery,   10
Gay, to manoeuvres, thudding by.
Spur and gun and limber plate
Flashed in the sun. Alert, elate,
Noble horses, foam at lip,
Harness, stirrup, holster, whip,   15
She watched the sun-tanned soldiery,
Till dust-white hedge had hidden away –
Its din into a rumour thinned –
The laughing, jolting, wild array:
And then – the wonder and tumult gone –   20
Stood nibbling a green leaf, alone,
Her dark eyes, dreaming . . . She turned, and ran,
Elf-like, into the house again.
The hare had vanished . . . 'Mother,' she said,

Her tear-stained cheek now flushed with red,   25
'Please, may I go and see it skinned?'

from *Memory and Other Poems* (1938)

Theresa Whistler dates the events depicted in 'Dry August Burned' to August 1910, when the de la Mare family were holidaying at the cottage in West Harting in West Sussex, within walking distance of the Thomas family. Their stay coincided with that of fifteen hundred troops on manoeuvres, which gave the family a foretaste of the militarisation of the country that would come with the First World War, and of Edward Thomas the artillery officer. It was, according to Whistler, the ten-year-old Florence de la Mare who, having cried at seeing a dead hare, ran out and was captivated by the soldiers.[1] Whistler also believes the poem to have been composed at the time of the events it depicts, but I doubt this is correct.[2] De la Mare isn't a diaristic poet and would often write of events years after they happened, when their full significance had become clear and could be shaped poetically (see, for instance, 'Sotto Voce'). 'Dry August Burned' is quite unlike any poem in The Listeners or Peacock Pie, but it does have the short story-like style, the brutality of subject matter and pessimism about modern humanity and its cruelties that is the hallmark of a number of poems from Memory (1938), the collection in which it first appeared. As I can find no manuscript evidence to date it earlier than that volume, I would suggest that 'Dry August Burned' is a poem of the mid-to-late 1930s.

The strange and arresting title appeared at proof stage. August was, until 1993 when the practice was banned, the time of stubble burning.[3] The fires would cause panicked hares to break cover and run from the flames and smoke, more so in a dry summer when fires often spread out of control. Readers in the 1930s would naturally have thought of the dry, hot August of 1914, the month of the outbreak of the First World War, and de la Mare appears to be cultivating the assumption from the reader that the poem is set in 1914.

Prior to being called 'Dry August Burned', the poem was called 'The Hare'. There is also a poem of that name in *Songs of Childhood* (1902), which provides a key to what happens within 'Dry August Burned':

'The Hare'

> In the black furrow of a field
> I saw an old witch-hare this night;
> And she cocked a lissome ear,
> And she eyed the moon so bright,
> And she nibbled of the green;
> And I whispered 'Whsst! witch-hare,'
> Away like a ghostie o'er the field
> She fled, and left the moonlight there.

(C.P., p. 6)

When de la Mare included 'The Hare' in his 1939 anthology *Animal Stories*, he let it stand as preface to a tale called 'The Witch Hare'. The rural speaker has been 'out thracking hares'. He then shoots a female hare, follows the track of its blood, 'whist, whisper – right up to Katey MacShane's door'. And there it seems to have taken on the shape of a woman who, when asked of her wound, merely says that it was cut with a reaping hook.[4] Hares were on de la Mare's mind again at the end of the 1930s. The early story 'In the Forest', which features a male hare and soldiers, was dug out and collected in *Stories, Essays and Poems* (1939). *Memory* (1938) also includes the poem 'A Hare', which reflects on man's enmity to the beast, its sympathy resting with the hare. Indeed, de la Mare's increasingly dark view of humankind is matched by his ever-stronger sympathy with the animal world. The poem before 'Dry August Burned' in *Memory* is 'Reserved', a bitter indictment of the whole industrial-utilitarian approach to animals and the way of living it has created.

The girl in 'Dry August Burned' is depicted in the terms of a shape-shifting witch-hare. In a trial for witchcraft in 1662, the Scottish woman Isobel Gowdie declared that to turn into a hare she would chant:

> I sall gae intil a hare,
> Wi' sorrow and sych and meickle care;
> And I sall gae in the Devillis name,
> Ay quhill I com hom againe.

[I shall go into a hare,/ With sorrow and sigh and much care;/ And shall go in the Devil's name,/ In a while I'll come home again]

To change back, she would say:

> Haire, haire, God send thee caire.
> I am in a hairis likness just now,
> Bot I sall be in a womanis likenes evin now.[5]

[Hare, hare, God send thee care./ I am in a hare's likeness
just now,/ But I shall be in a woman's likeness even now.]

At the opening of 'Dry August Burned', the girl runs out 'like
a leveret' (l. 8), a young hare. She has identified so strongly
with the hare that has been killed that she becomes a young
hare herself. At the end of the poem, she, like the witch-hare
in 'The Hare', nibbles of the green before running 'Elf-like'
(l. 23) back into the house. The hare has 'vanished' (l. 24). By
the end of the poem the girl has changed again, not into an
innocent child among the beasts but into a bloodthirsty one,
no longer able to sympathise with animal or, by implication,
human victims.

The reason for the change in her must be the presence of
the soldiers. The 'sun-tanned' young men (l. 16) may have
taken her from childhood innocence by awakening in her a
sexual attraction. But as much as the look of them, it is the
noise they make, the '*clop* of hoofs,/ the clang of dangling
chain, voices that rang' (ll. 6–7), that has enchanted her.

The whole sound world of the poem is unusual. The rhyme
scheme is irregular, some rhymes being adjacent; others are
a long way apart – notably 'artillery' (l. 10) and 'soldiery'
(l. 16), and 'thinned' (l. 18) and 'skinned' (l. 26). De la
Mare uses internal rhyme and near rhyme – for instance,
'gun' (l. 12) with 'sun' (l. 13) 'din' and 'thinned' (l. 18), yet
each time 'ran' appears as an (uncharacteristic) half-rhyme
(l. 8 and l. 22). The overall effect is something between de
la Mare's more usual music of enchantment and the jarring
pararhymes found in the war poems of Wilfred Owen.

Incantation

Vervain . . . basil . . . orison –
Whisper their syllablings till all meaning is gone,
And sound all vestige loses of mere word . . .
'Tis then as if, in some far childhood heard,
A wild heart languishing at the call of a bird,   5
Crying through ruinous windows, high and fair,
A secret incantation on the air:
A language lost; which, when its accents cease,
Breathes, voiceless, of a pre-Edenic peace.

from *Memory and Other Poems* (1938)

De la Mare was interested in the possible consciousness-altering effects of poetic sound. In *Come Hither*, he writes that there are 'many ways of reading verse aloud – one of them being with little change of pitch, and resembling a spoken chaunt, or "intoning". This drowses the waking mind; and the words resemble an incantation.'[1] The word 'incantation', though indicating words to be spoken or intoned, shares its root with 'enchantment', as de la Mare well knew (see notes to 'A Song of Enchantment'; introducing Shakespeare's songs, de la Mare writes: 'the Songs are incantations: they were intended to be sung').[2]

Readers are being directed to repeat the words '*Vervain* . . . *basil* . . . *orison*' until 'all meaning is gone': that is, these words should be deployed as a mantra and repeated until a state of altered consciousness is reached. But while those who do so may well experience the effects described in the poem, the words de la Mare has chosen do have meanings. In the language of flowers of the nineteenth century, 'Vervain' means enchantment. Used in rituals by Ancient Romans and druids alike, it continued to have a place in European popular remedies and folk culture. As Charlotte de la Tour's influential nineteenth-century study, *The Language of Flowers*, asserts, 'vervain is still among us, as it was among the ancients, the herb of incantation'.[3] Basil comes from the Greek for king, and is associated with the basilisk.[4] In I. A. Richards and C. K. Ogden's *The Meaning of Meaning*, whose contents de la Mare refers to in one of his lectures, it is recorded that the word 'Abracadabra' has been derived from Abraxas, originally the charm of the Basildean Gnostics, so this may be Basildean basil.[5] Orison is comparatively straightforward: with an ety-mology connecting it to speech rather than song, it is a form of prayer, and a reminder that incantations have been a devo-tional practice associated with all the major world religions – the unceasing repetition of the Jesus Prayer by ascetics would be an example of its place in the Christian tradition. The poem links the mantra-like recitation of words until they lose meaning and the reattainment of a 'pre-Edenic' state (l. 9), which is something of a paradox. If you take the Bible story literally, there was no human time before Eden. But then, from the point of view of the poem, in Eden man is already fallen, for it was there that Adam gave names to creation, and by giving it words separated himself from the sort of sounds the birds make.

Similar connections between mantra, language and bird-song to those de la Mare conjures in 'Incantation' are ex-plored by the philosopher Frits Staal in his 1990 study *Rules without Meaning*. Staal finds much in common between Vedic mantras and birdsong, as well as the speech of babies before they properly acquire language, and he hypothesises that the date of the oldest Vedic chants may predate the origin of lan-guage for communication. Staal also maintains:

Certain sorts of repetitions and refrain-like structures that seem to be common to both mantras and bird songs, are entirely absent from the syntax of ordinary language. In fact, any linguist who is familiar with syntactic structures cannot fail to be struck by the absence in almost all such structures of the typical repetitive features of both

233

mantras and bird songs. There is an area of overlap:
the domain of poetry. However, poetry seems in several
respects to constitute an intermediary area between
mantras and ordinary language.[6]

If there is an answer to why particular bird cries should have
given de la Mare such a profound intuition of the ruined state
humans find themselves in, the state of self and sound he has
lost and his poetry's connection to them, it must be some-
thing akin to this.

'Incantation', its ruinousness and birdsong, is strongly rem-
iniscent of a couple of passages in de la Mare's prose fiction.
In his story 'The Bird of Travel' (see notes to 'The Listeners'):

And then, while I was slowly returning towards it once
more, under the still, reddish, evening sky, suddenly I
heard thrice repeated an extraordinary call. It pierced my
mind like an arrow. It almost absurdly startled me – like
the shrilling of a decoy, as if my own name had been called
in a strange or forgotten tongue.

Of English birds, the blackcap, perhaps, sings with a
vestige of that wild and piercing sweetness. Imagine such
a voice twenty times more vigorous suddenly breaking in
upon that evening silence – falling on from note to note as
if some unearthly traveller were summoning from afar his
strayed dog on the hill side! [. . .] Here was the deserted
house, and still echoing in my heart that cry, the lure, as of
some innocent Banshee.[7]

From roughly the same period, comes this passage from *The Return* (1910):

> Hill and wailing cry and barn and water faded out. And he
> was staring as if in an endless stillness at an open window
> against which the sun was beating in a bristling torrent
> of gold, while out of the garden beyond came the voice
> of some evening bird singing with such an unspeakable
> ecstasy of grief it seemed it must be perched upon
> the confines of another world. The light gathered to a
> radiance almost intolerable, driving back with its raining
> beams some memory, forlorn, remorseless, remote.[8]

Both passages frame an experience that seems beyond words.

Brueghel's Winter

Jagg'd mountain peaks and skies ice-green
Wall in the wild cold scene below.
Churches, farms, bare copse, the sea
In freezing quiet of winter show;
Where ink-black shapes on fields in flood   5
Curling, skating, and sliding go.
To left, a gabled tavern; a blaze;
Peasants; a watching child; and lo,
Muffled, mute – beneath naked trees
In sharp perspective set a-row –   10
Trudge huntsmen, sinister spears aslant,
Dogs snuffling behind them in the snow;
And arrowlike, lean, athwart the air
    Swoops into space a crow.

But flame, nor ice, nor piercing rock,   15
Nor silence, as of a frozen sea,
Nor that slant inward infinite line
Of signboard, bird, and hill, and tree,
Give more than subtle hint of him
Who squandered here life's mystery.   20

from *Memory and Other Poems* (1938)

The Brueghel of 'Brueghel's Winter' is Pieter Breughel (or Bruegel) the Elder (*c.*1525-1569). His oil on wood painting of *Winter*, often referred to as *Hunters in the Snow*, dates from 1565 and is one of five paintings to survive from a series of pictures he painted on the theme of the seasons. The original painting hangs in the Kunsthistorisches Museum in Vienna, and was almost certainly not seen by de la Mare. He did, however, have a reproduction of the painting upon his wall, probably acquired following a letter sent to him by the painter Sir William Nicholson (1872–1949) on 13 May 1936, in which Nicholson says that if he had to choose one painting he would choose a good reproduction of Brueghel's *Winter*.[1] Nicholson sketches the painting in his letter, pointing out some of the details.

De la Mare's choice of vocabulary in the poem attunes itself to painting: 'ink-black' (l. 5) is alert to the use of pigment; 'perspective' (l. 10) uses the word in the usual sense but also as a term for a painter's rendering of three-dimensional space; 'sinister' (l. 11) plays on the word's origin in the Latin for 'left': the spears are ominous but they also point left and are on the left side of the painting. The description of the icy scene within the painting and its 'freezing quiet' (l. 4) subtly transforms into a description of the soundless and still condition of painting itself and its 'silence as of a frozen sea' (l. 16).

Some of the vocabulary is, in more senses than one, 'pointed': 'Jagg'd mountain peaks' (l. 1), 'sharp perspective' (l. 10) and 'arrowlike' (l. 13), the features of the described landscape taking on the characteristics of the spears of the huntsmen. As rhymes such as 'Tit for Tat' in *Peacock Pie* and 'Hi' in *Poems for Children* (1930) attest, de la Mare detested the cruelty of hunting. That he could also connect cruelty to animals with forebodings of war is made clear by the depiction of hare and soldier in 'Dry August Burned'.

If one maps out the lines at the end of 'Brueghel's Winter', the 'infinite line' (l. 17) shows itself to be a cross formed between 'signboard, bird, and hill, and tree' (l. 18); the bird itself (the crow) is also cross-like. This would indicate that the 'him' in the poem must be Jesus Christ; the hunters in the snow are his torturers and killers. Other subtle hints of Christ in the picture not explicitly referred to in the poem include a central bramble, which may allude to the crown of thorns, three 'naked' (l. 9) trees on the hill, which may allude to the three crosses at Golgotha and, so small that it may not have been easy to detect on de la Mare's reproduction, a tiny cross between the antlers of the deer on the sign at the front of the inn (in the painting, this must allude to St Hubert, the patron saint of hunters). De la Mare's Christian faith waxed and waned over the years, and how far 'Breughel's Winter' is or isn't a Christian poem will be a question of interpretation. Is 'squandered here' (l. 20) a reproach for giving up life's mystery, or a respectful Christian acknowledgement of Christ's self-sacrifice? In 'Brueghel's Winter' de la Mare is, as he is so often, no friend to definitive interpretation. Not mentioning Christ by name, he has also made it possible for the reader to come up with the less likely, but still plausible, identification of 'him' not as being Christ but Brueghel and 'here' being not Earth, but the painting itself.

Within a few years of the publication of 'Brughel's Winter', a number of eminent English and American poets, including Randall Jarrell, John Berryman and William Carlos Williams, wrote poems addressing paintings by Brueghel, including his *Winter/Hunters in the Snow*. The direct cause of this upsurge of poetic interest in the Renaissance painter was the disquisition on Breughel paintings in W. H. Auden's poem 'Musée des Beaux Arts', but de la Mare's poem predates, and may well have partly inspired, Auden's, which was written in December 1938, the year of the appearance of de la Mare's poem in *Memory*. The detail of the hunters' 'sinister' spears next to the 'snuffling dogs' in 'Breughel's Winter' anticipates the dogs and torturer's horse in Auden's poem and may explain how Auden's poem about the Musée de Beaux Arts in Brussels has on its mind a picture which hangs in Vienna.

'Brueghel's Winter' was not the only inspiration de la Mare gave to Auden. De la Mare's 1923 anthology *Come Hither* was, according to Auden, the book which 'more than any book I have read before or since taught me what poetry is'.[2] Its good yet catholic taste, its 'lack of literary class consciousness' and its knowledge that 'poetry does not have to be great or even serious to be good' were the touchstone for Auden's own anthologising.[3] It also ensured that Auden's poetry was shaped more deeply by Georgian, or at least de la Mare's, taste than it was by the modernism he imbibed a few years later. The influence of de la Mare's own poems on Auden's verse is discernible too: in his strangers, questers and travellers and in his poems asking questions or listening for sounds, including 'O Where Are You Going?' and 'O What Is That Sound?'; it can also be heard in the music of some of his lyrics. Auden's large debt to de la Mare was repaid, first in appreciative reviews of de la Mare's books and, after de la Mare's death, in Auden's introduction and selection of *A Choice of de la Mare's Verse* (1963).

Swallows Flown

Whence comes that small continuous silence
   Haunting the livelong day?
This void, where a sweetness, so seldom heeded,
   Once ravished my heart away?
As if a loved one, too little valued,   5
   Had vanished – could not stay?

from *Memory and Other Poems* (1938)

Mournings and ghosts need not be the grand affairs of formal elegies, tombstones or haunted houses; de la Mare is just as good on smaller absences, the traces in which we feel lives and happenings no longer there. In this poem it is the absence of the sound of swallows, which arrive in England in April or May and are gone in September or October and were the background noise between spring and autumn when the de la Mares were living at Taplow. This noise gradually changes. It is originally the chatter of the nesting pair, which swells as their chicks are hatched and grow and diminishes when they are fledged. In listening to the sound of swallows, de la Mare has been listening to the coming into being, growing and dispersal of a family. Perhaps this family reminded him of his own: by the 1930s, de la Mare's offspring had (with the partial exception of his youngest son Colin) flown the nest, but there were now grandchildren to pay visits and to leave again.

The asides – 'so seldom heeded' (l. 3), 'too little valued' (l. 5) – and the pause between 'vanished' and 'could not stay' (l. 6) are finely judged, small notes of inconspicuous regret. Why 'could not stay'? Because the narrator made the loved one go? Because the loved one died? Or simply because, like the swallows quitting the English autumn, the time had come for the loved one to go.

The word 'livelong' (l. 2), which means 'entire', has nothing to do with 'lifelong' but comes in origin from the Middle English word '*lef*', meaning 'dear' or 'beloved', and so is here manifesting that desire to love every moment, and in particular every moment given to us by the natural world, that we find in a poem such as 'Fare Well'.

We do not know what loved one the author has in mind: 'ravished my heart away' (l. 4) may imply the disappearance of someone who was once the object of romantic love or merely what it directly states, that the swallows took the poet's heart away when they travelled south. The fact that 'Swallows Flown' is placed next to 'Sallie's Musical Box' (see notes for 'Sallie') in the 1942 edition of de la Mare's *Collected Poems* might suggest that the poem conceals, as 'Sallie's Musical Box' may conceal, a sigh for the passing of the lyric muse. If so, it would be an odd sentiment to voice, for the music of 'Swallows Flown' is, to my mind and ear, every bit as beautiful as that of the early lyrics. The last two lines are reminiscent of Thomas Hardy's poems, particularly on the death of his wife, 'vanished – could not stay' (l. 6) being, perhaps, small euphemisms for a greater and more permanent departure, but they are particularly apposite to swallows, which often nest in chimneys, under the eaves of houses or in other suitable corners, fellow residents who must suddenly depart.

The Old Summerhouse

This blue-washed, old, thatched summerhouse –
Paint scaling, and fading from its walls –
How often from its hingeless door
I have watched – dead leaf, like the ghost of a mouse,
Rasping the worn brick floor –   5
The snows of the weir descending below,
And their thunderous waterfall.

Fall – fall: dark, garrulous rumour,
Until I could listen no more.
Could listen no more – for beauty with sorrow   10
Is a burden hard to be borne:
The evening light on the foam, and the swans, there;
That music, remote, forlorn.

from *Memory and Other Poems* (1938)

'The Old Summerhouse' is a place where de la Mare's long-established preoccupations with old buildings, small sounds, hauntedness and natural enchantments all meet. A summerhouse is a sort of garden hut designed to enable one to sit out on hot days. But while this is, I presume, a poem of summer, a sense of summers gone washes over summer present, with that dead leaf and the fading paint.

The sound and sense are almost still at first. Clusters of naturally stressed syllables around those bearing the metre slow the line. Small, very particular visual details detain the eye. 'Scaling', 'fading' (l. 2), the motion of a leaf over a floor whose brick has already been worn by other things, other leaves, other people who have come to sit here, other visits by the poem's narrator: everything in the summerhouse is being slowly washed away.

Then comes the break and the rush. The division between the stanzas mimics the falling of water over the weir, a thunderous sound that falls away into a more distant 'garrulous rumour' (l. 8) through further echoes and finally into 'That music remote, forlorn' (l. 13). This marked change between stanzas is reminiscent of the traditional turn, or *volta*, that comes when one reaches the last six lines of a sonnet.

The hypnotic effect of the sound of water descending down weirs exerted a great force over de la Mare and his imagination. In his 1910 novel *The Return*, the hero looks out on a river:

So absorbed he became as he stood leaning over the wooden sill above the falling water, that eye and ear became enslaved by the roar and stillness. And in the faint atmosphere of age that seemed like a veil to hang about the odd old house and these prodigious branches, he fell into a kind of waking dream.[1]

De la Mare reports something similar when writing to Naomi Royde-Smith of a time he spent in March 1913 by the Frome with Edward Thomas, feeling his wits 'slipping away in the enormous roar of the falling water. I didn't want to *be* anything but *that*.'[2]

The poet Peter Scupham has commented that 'Orsino might have written "The Old Summerhouse", or Feste sung the second stanza to him.'[3] There is something of the melancholy Duke and the sad, singing fool of Shakespeare's *Twelfth Night* here, and I think Orsino's opening speech on music can be distantly heard behind de la Mare's lines:

> That strain again! – it had a dying fall:
> O, it came o'er my ear like the sweet sound
> That breathes upon a bank of violets
> Stealing and giving odour! Enough; no more:
> 'Tis not so sweet now as it was before.

Along with Orsino listening to music, one can just make out Keats listening to his nightingale, envisioning:

> Charm'd magic casements, opening on the foam
> Of perilous seas, in faery lands forlorn.

> Forlorn! the very word is like a bell
> To toll me back from thee to my sole self![4]

Whether to call these influences or deliberate allusions is hard to say, and probably beside the point; they function as both. Echoes of such well-loved lines may sound through de la Mare's words almost automatically, yet they are also a part of his understanding of the world. They allow the view and sounds of the old summerhouse to open not just onto the weir downstream but onto the lands of Illyria and Faerie. Orsino appears to be melancholy for music alone, as does the speaker of 'The Old Summerhouse'. Yet in *Twelfth Night*, his speech on music foreshadows Viola's mourning for her drowned brother, Sebastian. The beauty and sorrow of 'The Old Summerhouse' never mentions death and nor does it detail times past or the people who have lived and visited this place, but its sense of time passing like vast waters over the weir brings both to mind.

'Of a Son'

A garish room – oil-lamped; a stove's warm blaze;
Gilt chairs drawn up to candles, and green baize:
The doctor hastened in – a moment stayed,
Watching the cards upon the table played –
Club, and sharp diamond, and heart, and spade.   5
And – still elated – he exclaimed, '*Parbleu*,
A thousand pardons, friends, for keeping you;
I feared I'd never see the lady through.
A boy, too! *Magnifique* the fight she made!
Ah, well, she's happy now!' Said one, '"She"? – who?' 10
    'A woman called Landru.'

Gentle as flutter of dove's wing, the cards
Face downwards fell again; and fever-quick,
Topped by old Time and scythe, a small brass clock
In the brief hush of tongues resumed its tick.   15

from *Memory and Other Poems* (1938)

A doctor is late to a card game. He pauses a moment to watch the other players at the 'green baize' (l. 2) that covers the card table to prevent the underside of the cards from being reflected or from sliding when dealt. The doctor, who is presumably a Frenchman (one may be tempted to give the French words an English pronunciation, but presumably '*Parbleu*' (l. 6), a euphemism for '*Par Dieu*' or 'By God', is intended to rhyme with 'Landru' (l. 11) rather than 'you' (l. 7)) excuses himself by saying that he has been detained by a lady and a boy and that the lady put up a fight that was '*Magnifique*' (l. 9). On being asked by one of the card players who this lady is, the doctor says she is called 'Landru' (l. 11). The clock, which seemed to have stopped ticking, starts again, and there is a new deal of cards.

More appears to be going on than first meets the eye. Why does the poem have such a curious title, and why is it in quotation marks? What manner of fight has the lady has been making? Who is the boy? And why, in a poem by a writer who usually reserves surnames for epitaphs, are we pointedly given this lady's surname?

There is also the question of the card game. A gilt-chaired social setting and four cards played in succession suggest this is a game of contract bridge. When it comes to the impenetrability of its rules for the uninitiated, bridge is up there with cricket and the Japanese tea ceremony, but I shall try to make clear what is going on.

Bridge is conventionally played by four players divided into two teams of two. There is an initial bidding process between all four players to decide which suit will be 'trumps'; the highest-bidding pair will also declare how many 'tricks' they believe they will make. After the bidding process is concluded, one player drops out, leaving their partner to play their hand, which becomes what is termed 'the dummy'. There is also a variant of the game with a 'revolving dummy', which I suspect is what is being played when the doctor arrives. As the hand is played, one card from each player's hand put down in turn constitutes 'a trick'. Players must follow suit if they can and if they cannot, players put down a card of a different suit. Since the game is played with 'trumps', if this card is in the suit which happens to have been nominated as trumps, that player will win the trick regardless of whatever the nominal suit of that trick is, assuming that no trump card of higher value is subsequently put down. In the poem, the cards are about to be dealt again, so the succession of four cards we see in line 5 is the last trick of this particular deal, making the fact that all play cards of different suits perfectly likely. If that is the case, the value of any particular card will make no difference to the result of this trick. What the winning card is will depend on which trump was successfully bid for at the opening of the hand, or whether the winning bid was, in fact, 'no trump'.

All this gives us five possible solutions to this particular trick. Not coincidentally, I can also find five possible solutions to the mystery of this poem's plot, and, as at least two of them seem linked to the possible 'bids' determining the outcome of the hand, I'll arrange them accordingly:

1. Clubs.
After a magnificent fight for life, a lady has died 'of a son' in childbirth. The doctor's phrase 'she's happy now' (l. 10),

implies that, after the struggle, the lady is now in heaven. Her son survives her. One person dies.

2. Diamonds

This is 'sharp' (l. 5) diamonds. De la Mare was addicted to the details of grisly murder cases and used this knowledge to explore similar territory in some of his writing, which included a never-to-be-performed dark melodrama of the 1920s, alternatively titled *Dr Fleet* and *The Lady Killer*. The lady's name is 'Landru', the surname of the notorious French serial killer, the 'real-life Bluebeard', Henri Désiré Landru (1869–1922). Landru seduced affluent widows who answered his adverts in lonely hearts columns. He would then gain control of their wealth before murdering and dismembering them, burning their corpses. In 1921, Landru stood trial on eleven counts of murder committed between 1914 and 1919. Landru's first victim was thirty-nine-year-old Jeanne Cuchet, who had a sixteen-year-old son.[1]

The plot of this reading of '"Of a Son"' leads to us to conclude that a lady and a boy have been killed by the doctor, perhaps for her diamonds: despite the fight, he has seen her 'through' (l. 8). It is the bodies of a lady and 'Of a Son' which have been left. Two people die.

3. Hearts

The attentive doctor has seen a lady through a difficult labour: she has been successfully delivered 'Of a son' (l. 9), leaving us with a happy mother and a heart-warming ending. No one dies, and there is one more person in the world.

4. Spades.

An unsuccessful labour has led to the death of a mother and 'A boy too!' (see '1. Clubs'). Two people die.

5. No Trump

All the above 'trumps' are plausible, but in bridge, a fifth possible option is available: that of bidding for and having 'no trump'. (In a real game of bridge, this would mean that the player putting down the club would be the winner). The least satisfactory part of '2. Diamonds' is that it is the lady who is called Landru. Landru may have partnered his victims, but he did so under aliases, so why is the lady named Landru, unless to imply that it is she rather than the doctor who is a killer?

We may have missed some further clues. The room is 'garish' (l. 1) and there is a blazing stove. The doctor is 'still elated' (l. 6) when he joins the company. When the cards are dealt again, they fall 'fever-quick,/ Topped by old Time and scythe' (l. 13–14). The lady has not been in labour at all and nor has the doctor killed her; rather he has been nursing her through a perilous fever. Fortunately, the lady has put up a tremendous fight and he has 'seen her through', and 'a boy too', but in doing so the doctor has caught the fever himself. Both boy and lady live. Time and its scythe are waiting for the card players. It seems likely that the death toll will in fact be four.

The House

A lane at the end of Old Pilgrim Street
Leads on to a sheep-track over the moor,
Till you come at length to where two streams meet,
The brook called Liss, and the shallow Stour.

Their waters mingle and sing all day –   5
Rushes and kingcups, rock and stone;
And aloof in the valley, forlorn and gray,
Is a house whence even the birds have flown.

Its ramshackle gate swings crazily; but
No sickle covets its seeding grass;   10
There's a cobbled path to a door close-shut;
But no face shows at the window-glass.

No smoke wreathes up in the empty air
From the chimney over its weed-green thatch;
Briar and bryony ramble there;   15
And no thumb tirls at the broken latch.

Even the warbling water seems
To make lone music for none to hear;
Else is a quiet found only in dreams,
And in dreams this foreboding, though not of fear.   20

Yes, often at dusk-fall when nearing home –
The hour of the crescent and evening star –
Again to the bridge and the streams I come,
Where the sedge and the rushes and kingcups are:

And I stand, and listen, and sigh – in vain;   25
Since only of Fancy's the face I see;
Yet its eyes in the twilight on mine remain,
And it seems to be craving for company.

from *Bells and Grass: A Book of Rhymes* (1941)

I have been unable to find the place where a brook called the Liss crosses the River Stour near an 'Old Pilgrim Street'. If such a location does exist, I would expect to find it close to the village of Chilham near Canterbury in Kent, where the ancient track known as the Pilgrim's Way runs by the Stour. There is also a River Stour in Dorset, which appears in poems by Thomas Hardy including 'Overlooking the River Stour', but the reference to Old Pilgrim Street would suggest that that is not the Stour referred to here.

The Pilgrim's Way took on great significance for writers of de la Mare's generation. Running from Winchester to Canterbury and providing a picturesque alternative to the built-up and busy route from London to Canterbury taken by Chaucer's pilgrims, the Pilgrim's Way is hymned and mythologised in Hilaire Belloc's *The Old Road* (1904); it and other ancient walkways were to be walked and written about by Edward Thomas. Interest in the Pilgrim's Way would reach an even larger public three years after this poem's publication, with the release of the Powell and Pressburger film *A Canterbury Tale* in 1944.

The name of the brook may owe more to autobiographical resonance than to geographical exactitude. The village of Liss is near to West Harting, where de la Mare and his family spent summers during his writing of *The Listeners* and *Peacock Pie*, as well as to Steep, the East Hampshire village where Thomas lived for a number of years. Liss also happens to be near the beginning of the Pilgrim's Way, if not the River Stour. Those chasing up a connection with Thomas will also find slight similarities to his story 'The Pilgrim', although its Pilgrim's

Way is the one from London to St Davids in Wales and its brook is the Alan, and to descriptions of old houses, one of them beside the Pilgrim's Way, to be found in Thomas's *The South Country* (1909).[1]

Though it has a style and feel akin to poems in the later adult volumes, 'The House' was included in de la Mare's 1941 children's volume *Bells and Grass* and brings to mind a rhyme from *Peacock Pie*:

The Old Stone House

Nothing on the grey roof, nothing on the brown,
Only a little greening where the rain drops down;
Nobody at the window, nobody at the door,
Only a little hollow which a foot once wore;
But still I tread on tiptoe, still tiptoe on I go,   5
Past nettles, porch, and weedy well, for oh, I know
A friendless face is peering, and a clear still eye
Peeps closely through the casement as my step goes by.

'The Old Stone House', with its trepidatious zest, vivid details and 'Wee Willie Winkie' rhythm tiptoes around a house the later poem views sedately from afar. The everyday 'ghost', the 'little hollow which a foot once wore', becomes – in imagination? in actuality? – that ghost-like face at the window, with its 'clear still eye' (l. 7).

In the later poem, it may not just be the house but the pilgrim de la Mare that is now old. The garden, through lack of a scythe, seems to be missing the tidying of the gardener, death.

Even if there is 'Nobody at the window' (l. 3) of 'The Old Stone House', the narrator of the earlier rhyme completely believed in the face there; the narrator of 'The House' can only sigh that 'only of Fancy's the face I see' (l. 26).

In 'The House', the capitalisation of Fancy's initial letter suggests that de la Mare has in mind the definition of the word put forward by Samuel Taylor Coleridge (1772–1834) in his *Biographia Literaria*. For Coleridge, Fancy is a lesser thing than the mysterious power of the Imagination: more consciously willed, 'a mode of Memory emancipated from the order of time and space'.[2] If that is what de la Mare has in mind, it is tempting to read the Liss as representing Imagination and the Shallow Stour as Fancy.

During the First World War, de la Mare stopped writing poetry for a time, remarking in a letter to Naomi Royde-Smith: 'it's impossible to turn out a nursery jingle unless some queer little door's ajar in one's mind, somebody's peeping in the window at me.'[3] The uncanny appearance of the face in the window where no face should be has become emblematic of poetic inspiration.

The 'kingcups' (l. 6) look like giant buttercups and are also known as 'marsh marigolds'. English 'bryony' (l. 15) is 'white bryony', a species of vigorous vine which bears white flowers and red berries. The word 'tirls' (l. 16) here means 'rattles'.

Dreamland

Annie has run down to the mill dam,
Annie is down by the weir;
Who was it calling her name, then?
Nobody else to hear?
Cold the water, calm and deep,   5
Honey-sweet goldilocks half-asleep,
Where the green-grey willows weep,
Annie is down by the weir.

from *Bells and Grass: A Book of Rhymes* (1941)

At first sight, 'Dreamland' is a pretty, if pretty conventional, nursery piece: the willows weep as willows will and there is even a delightful little goldilocks. Yet stay with the rhyme a moment and there are aspects of the poem which may puzzle and then trouble. Who or what is calling Annie? Does this voice mean her well? Is it merely in Annie's imagination? Is she a half-asleep child hearing voices in the falling water? The waters are cold and deep, but are we looking at Annie looking down upon the water or up from it? Are we looking through the reflected eyes of a girl in love with her own reflection or staring into the Other World? And what if these willows are not just weeping for convention's sake? What if something has caused their weeping? That second 'Annie is down by the weir' may mean that Annie has run to be beside the weir. But given that we now have the impression of a girl more *in* the water than above it, there is a hint that something has happened to the half-asleep child who is hearing voices. Annie may be down in the waters, rather than down beside them.

Annie is reminiscent of Ann, the seven-year-old girl and youngest of the three sisters, who is abducted by the fairies in *Crossings: A Fairy Play*, which de la Mare wrote with the composer Cecil Armstrong Gibbs and staged in an all-boy school production of 1919: 'Her hair is parted in the middle, and severely plaited on either side of her smooth round cheeks. It is of the rarest, faintest tines of gold.'[1] She also brings to mind the youngest of the three sisters in 'Reflections'. But it is the fate of another 'Annie', the protagonist of 'Down-Adown-Derry', a rhyme first in *Songs of Childhood* and which went on to supply the title of de la Mare's 1922 book of fairy poems that may provide the biggest clue to the mysterious, elliptical lyric of 'Dreamland'. In the poem, 'Sweet Annie Maroon' is 'Gathering daisies' by the Mill, where 'waters go brawling', when she sees a fairy who bids her 'Come to my water-house' in the sea. Annie appears to answer the call and the poem finishes with her bereft father searching for her:

> He may call o'er the water,
> Cry – cry through the Mill,
> But Annie Maroon, alas!
> Answer ne'er will

The child reading or listening may think Annie has gone away with the fairies to wear seaweed and coral in their undersea kingdom; an adult will think she has drowned, her body disappeared only because it has drifted downstream. The suspicion is that the Annie of 'Dreamland' and the Annie of 'Down-Adown-Derry' are one and the same person.

The poem 'Dreamland' first appeared in the children's collection *Bells and Grass* (the title of the collection was borrowed from 'Eve', a poem by de la Mare's friend Ralph Hodgson). In its introduction, de la Mare correctly described *Bells and Grass* as 'the last' book 'of its kind that I shall have the opportunity of making'. That opportunity was a gift from de la Mare's younger to his elder self:

About a year ago, I was looking through a jackdaw jumble of old papers and old letters – the contents of a packing case, a Tate sugar-box, which had been left undisturbed,

I think, since 1924 [. . .] among a few old manuscripts in the box I came across a commonplace book, bound in black leather. It had been mysteriously forgotten; yet at a glimpse, its contents at once came welling up into memory again. About twenty-four pages of it had been crammed, top to bottom, with pencil scribblings, many of them dated 1905, the remainder of a date not later, I fancy, than 1906. Some of these were marked 'Copied'. And a few afterwards appeared in print. A few are still incompletely readable even by the writer of them![2]

The book is still preserved: the poems, and indeed the illegibility of some of the handwriting, are as de la Mare describes them. This confrontation with verses from the beginning of *Peacock Pie* allowed him to find again the poet he was. This was partly the acknowledged opportunity to have access to his childhood-remembering mind, and to the light, songlike lyricism that accompanied it. Yet many of the best poems in *Bells and Grass* are not outtakes from earlier volumes but poems written in older age, shadowed by de la Mare's earlier poems and younger self.

Sallie

When Sallie with her pitcher goes
Down the long lane where the hawthorn blows
    For water from the spring,
I watch her bobbing sun-bright hair,
In the green leaves and blossoms there,   5
Shining and gleaming primrose-fair;
Till back again, like bird on wing,
Her pitcher, brimmed, she turns to bring –
    Oh, what a joy to see!
And her clear voice, the birds' above,   10
Rings sweet with joy, entranced with love –
    Ah! would 'twere love for me!

from *Bells and Grass: A Book of Rhymes* (1941)

'Sallie' is a rhyme and a person that seems as natural and timeless as the blossom. Who is she? On the one hand, it might seem she is 'the darling of my heart/ And she lives in our alley', the girl who resides in the poem by Henry Carey (1687–1743). Yet de la Mare's Sallie is also something less day-to-day: an ideal of young love, Flora, the goddess of the flowers, a spirit of spring, her body at one with green leaves, her voice at one with the birds.

The name 'Sallie' crops up elsewhere in de la Mare. In *Crossings*, Sallie is 'a slim dark girl of seventeen or nineteen, with a dark mobile face'.[1] Sallie spends the play in the company of her younger brother and two younger sisters. After a bequest from an aunt, the children leave London to take charge of a haunted and fairy-visited house in the country. Things run out of control and the fairies abduct her sister Ann, though all ends well.

The hero of Robertson Davies's 1972 novel *The Manticore* is 'enchanted' by a school production of *Crossings* and falls helplessly in love with Sallie, whom he describes as being 'very much a de la Mare girl', as well as the young woman who plays her. But if some young men can't help falling in love with the Sallie in *Crossings*, Sallie has no young man on her mind. In the words of the musicologist Stephen Banfield: 'as Barrie's Peter Pan is isolated from the Darling family by his inability to grow up, so Sallie . . . is isolated from the perfunctory world of adults through her attachment to the Candlestickmaker, the "queer half human creature" who is "Dream, Romance, the other World" . . . de la Mare explained to Gibbs on sending him the *Crossings* scenario in

December 1918.'[2] Whether or not this explains what's on Sallie's mind in this poem, the suspicion is that she may be as much de la Mare's muse as she is an object of romantic reverie. The psychoanalyst Carl Jung would term such a figure an 'anima', the feminine inner personality in the male unconscious, which is doubtless the reason she turns up in *The Manticore* in the memories of a man undergoing Jungian psychoanalysis. De la Mare uses the term 'Anima' in *Behold, This Dreamer!*, where one of the sections is entitled 'Animus and Anima' (the animus being the anima's inverse), but quoting Paul Claudel and Henri Brémond rather than Jung – Brémond's anima is the feminine embodiment of the poetic imagination.

Memory and Other Poems (1938) has the quatrain:

Sallie's Musical Box

Once it made music, tiny, frail, yet sweet –
Bead-note of bird where earth and elfland meet.
Now its thin tinkling stirs no more, since she
Whose toy it was, has gone; and taken the key.

The lines are beautiful and suggestive in themselves, but the poem contributes to the impression that Sallie may have an identity as the begetter of the more tinkling verses in *Songs of Childhood* and *Peacock Pie*. Unfortunately, it also seems that she has taken her key and won't come back. Yet in the poems of *Bells and Grass*, there is Sallie, prettier than ever and not always dealing with childhood things.

What caused Sallie to drop by once more? There was, first of all, the finding of the commonplace book of old verses (see the notes to 'Dreamland'), but there was a flesh-and-blood stimulus as well. Nathalie Saxton had first met de la Mare in 1936 when she had the job of nursing him and his ailing wife (de la Mare had a bad case of the 'flu, but Elfie had begun the protracted decline from Parkinson's disease and other illnesses she would suffer in the years before her death in 1943). Saxton and de la Mare kept in contact and would meet in London. A different sort of 'de la Mare girl' – along with the large, attractive eyes and high cheekbones, she had weak health and sticking-out teeth – Saxton had little formal education but was sensible and kind, and evidently very fond of de la Mare. The two had an innocent affair: she took him to antique shops; he took her to St Paul's Churchyard; they laughed and sang songs in the park. Eventually Saxton's mother decided that such goings on were not quite respectable and made her daughter return the relationship to a friendly but professional footing. Saxton was to nurse de la Mare during his final years.

The House

The rusty gate had been chained and padlocked
    Against the grass-grown path,
Leading no-whither as I knew well,
    In a twilight still as death.

Once, one came to an old stone house there,   5
    Wheels crunched in those scarce-seen ruts;
A porch with jasmine, a stone-fringed garden –
    Lad's love, forget-me-nots.

A happy house in that long-gone sunshine;
    And a face in the glass-bright moon,   10
And a voice at which even memory falters,
    Now that the speaker's gone.

I watch that image as I look at the pathway –
    My once accustomed zest,
As the painted gate on its hinges opened,   15
    Now locked against the past!

A true face too, yet scant of the future –
    A book that I never read . . .
Nor shall now, since I soon must be going
    To another old house instead.   20

from *Inward Companion: Poems* (1950)

The title might indicate a rebuild of 'The House' from *Bells and Grass* (itself a poem which looks back to 'The Old Stone House'), and in some obvious ways it is. Yet here and elsewhere, such old houses prompt a new and increasingly layered picture from the older poet rather than an inferior imitation of his earlier work.

'The House' is a poem of past, present and future. Even the later, padlocked view is in the past; the paths lead 'no-whither' (to nowhere), 'as I knew well' (l. 3) not 'as I know well'. Since one no longer comes to an 'old stone house there' (l. 5), that house must have been destroyed: it is literally, and it seems also symbolically, the house of the past. The seeing of 'a face in the glass-bright moon' (l. 10) initially seems to be just the man in the moon, but it connects to 'a voice at which even memory falters' (l. 11). The narrator watches his old zestful self heading towards the brightly painted gate and the future. In addition to that imaginary face in the moon, the narrator also recalls a 'true face . . . scant of the future' (l. 17), a face which had little future left to it, so presumably soon to die after the moment of recollection. The 'book that I never read' (l. 18) must be the future.

Unusually for de la Mare, the poem not only employs half-rhyme but does so consistently. Following the logic of this, 'read' (l. 18) cannot be a full rhyme with 'instead' but is in the present tense and rhymes with 'seed'. And yet, at the end of a poem there can be a pressure to feel the closure of full rhyme, which if yielded to would put 'read' into the past. The ambiguity this creates allows the narrator to say both that he never foresaw what was to happen to the possessor of the 'true face' but also that he never reads the future now. Why? Because he must soon be going to 'another old house' (l. 20). This alludes not to 'The Old Stone House' but to another rhyme in *Peacock Pie*, 'The Old House' into which 'so many people go', though no one ever comes out.

The flowers of the house and its garden have names that are redolent of youth and times past. 'Jasmine' is usually a vine with white, sweet-smelling flowers, and though it can have romantic connotations, in the Victorian language of flowers it indicates 'amiableness'.[1] 'Lad's-love' has feathery green-grey leaves and is a herb of the sunflower family that gets its name from its supposed aphrodisiac properties. But while its words conjure youthful love, they may have other connotations here (see below). I suspect the forget-me-not is mentioned in order to indicate what its name says; nevertheless, in *Come Hither*, de la Mare writes:

> As for the '*Forget-me-not*', it is only within the last hundred years or so that this name has been applied to the Great Water Scorpion Grass. There is a legend from the German to account for its name. A knight in armour and his Lady were straying beside a deep and rapid river. She espied a pretty pale flower growing in midstream, and entreated the Knight to pluck her a spray of it. He leapt in and perished, having adjured her with his last breath, as he flung the spray toward the bank, '*Vergiss mein nicht!*' – Forget me not!
>
> But apart from the fact that this is the 'blue and bright-eyed flower of the *brook*,' and flourishes no more

in deep water than a sailor does on land; to some tastes, Mouse-ear, which is all that *Myosotis* means, may seem a better name for it than the sentimental one borrowed from abroad.[2]

If de la Mare does have a particular voice in mind – and while the 'voice' could be interpreted as his past self, such an interpretation doesn't strike me as likely – there are a number of candidates for its possessor. Elfrida de la Mare had died on 11 July 1943. De la Mare's early friend and mentor Mary Coleridge (1861–1907) wrote a poem entitled 'The Deserted House' and, though it borrows a title from Tennyson, the poem is a discernible influence on de la Mare's own deserted houses, particularly 'The Old Stone House' in *Peacock Pie*. As 'The Deserted House' is Coleridge's final completed poem and one which seems to figure death, it has a particular poignancy: from the start, writing about deserted houses may have been de la Mare's way of remembering her.

'The House' also brings to mind Edward Thomas. Not only were both poets lovers of old houses, but Thomas was de la Mare's teacher on plants. On one occasion Thomas sent de la Mare a box of roots and seeds, including forget-me-nots, for his garden.[3] Moreover, Thomas had lad's love growing in the gardens of his homes at Wick Green and Yew Tree Cottage.[4] The poem in which Thomas contemplates the herb is known by its other name, 'Old Man', but in it Thomas contemplates both names and their significance. 'Old Man' finishes with Thomas, who has been trying to remember its scent, failing to do so:

No garden appears, no path, no hoar-green bush
Of Lad's-love, or Old Man, no child beside,
Neither father nor mother, nor any playmate;
Only an avenue, dark, nameless, without end.[5]

Whether it is Thomas himself who is remembered or not, de la Mare is at least recalling Thomas's use of the herb's name and deploying a similar switching of temporal perspectives between the old man he is and the young man he once was.

Winged Chariot

'Is every subject apt for rambling rhyme? –
Some are intractable and some sublime:
Only Eternity could master Time.

'As I sat by myself, I talked to myself,
And myself replied to me . . .'

. . . Why this absurd concern with clocks, my friend?
Watching Time waste will bring no more to spend,
Nor can retard the inevitable end.

'I, whom thou seest
with horyloge
in hande,
Am naméd Tyme,
the lord of very
howre. . . .'

Yet when, the old wide staircase climbed once more,
Your bag in hand, you attain its second floor,   5
Turn the Yale key in lock, sigh, open the door

And into these familiar rooms you slip –
Where even Silence pauses, finger on lip –
Three emulous metal tongues you wake from sleep.

Do they suffice you? No, you pause again.   10
And (as if mechanisms made by men
The Truth could tell) you search each face. And then,

Though every minute of your life's your own,
Though here you are 'master' and at ease, alone –
You ring up *TIM*; consult the telephone.   15

The *telephone*! . . . Then, these precautions past,
Time made in Greenwich safely yours at last,
You set all three some fifteen minutes fast.

Psychopathist might guess the reason why
You indulge your wits in this mendacity.   20
Think *you* Man's 'enemy' is thus put by?

Think you so fleet a thing – that madcap hare
You daily waken from its nightlong lair –
Time, would consent such stratagems to share?

Or is it that you reassurance seek,   25
Deeming the Future will appear less bleak
Now that your clocks will 'go' a whole long week?

'. . . O, it came ore my eare, like the sweet sound That breathes upon a banke of Violets; Stealing, and giving odours . . .'

If Time's a stream – and we are told it's so,
Its peace were shattered if you check its flow;
What Naiad then ev'n fingertip would show? –   30
Her imaged other-world in ruins? . . . No:

Should once there haunt your too-attentive ear
A peevish pendulum, no more you'll hear
The soundless thunder of the distant weir

278

Which is Eternity . . . Blest reverie: 35
When, from the serfdom of this world set free,
The self a moment rapt in peace may be;

Not void; but poised, serene, 'twixt praise
    and prayer,
Such as the flower-clocked woods and
    meadows share,
Lulled and fed only by day's light and air.   40

How punctual they! But to no *tic-toc* rune.
Theirs is an older code than 'May' and 'June';
As testifies 'Jack-go-to-bed-at-noon';
Airiest of ghosts, he goes to bed at noon!

Nimbused in his own song at dawn of day,   45   *'. . . Jocund day
From earth's cold clods the skylark wings his way,   stands tiptoe on the
Into the sun-gilt crest of heaven to stray.   mistie mountaine's
                                                                                    top . . .'*

Housed in the dark of sleepy farms below,
At their own hour the cocks craned up to crow,
Their harems hearkening in obsequious row.   50

But wheel and barrel, ratchet, pawl, and spring?
Dear heart alive, how dull and dead a thing,
Compared with any creature on the wing,
Wherewith to measure even a glimpse of Spring.

Or, 'splitting seconds', to attempt to mete   55
The thrill with which a firefly's pinions beat.
Yes, or the languor, lingering and sweet,

When, lulled in the embraces of the sun,
The rose exults that her brief course is run
And heat-drowsed honey-bee has come;
   is gone.   60

Last night, at window idling, what saw I
Against the dusky summer greenery? –
Midges, a myriad, that up and down did fly,
Obedient to the breezes eddying by –
Sylphs scarcely of Time but of mere
   transciency: 65

An ovoid of intricated *winged* things, beautiful;
As on some sea-breeze morning, sunned and cool,
One may peer down upon a wavering shoal –
Like eddying weed in ebb-tide's lap and lull –
Of tiniest fish-fry in a rock-bound pool.   70

[. . .]

Yet, when, a child, I was content to rove
The shingled beach that I was Crusoe of,   220
All that I learned there was akin to love.

The glass-clear billow toppling on the sand,
Sweet salt-tanged air, birds, rock-drift – eye, ear, hand;
All was a language love could understand.

Yet there was mystery too: those steps of stone – 225   *'... Those steps of*
In the green paddock where I played alone –   *stone ...'*
    Cracked, weed-grown,
Where often allured my hesitant footsteps down

To an old sun-stained key-holed door that stood,
The guardian of an inner solitude,   230
Whereon I longed but dreaded to intrude;
Peering and listening as quietly as I could.

There, as I knew, in brooding darkness lay
The waters of a reservoir. But why –
In deadly earnest, though I feigned, in play –   235
Used I to stone those doors; then run away,
Listening enthralled in the hot sunny day

To echo and rumour; and that distant sigh,
As if some friend profaned had made reply, –
    When merely a child was I?   240

    [. . .]

Better than that, it were to stay the child   795
Before 'time' tamed you. When you both
     ran wild
And to heaven's *Angelus* were reconciled.

Host of all sun-blest thing by nature his,
His mind imagines all on earth he sees,
His heart a honey comb of far resemblances –
     Ere falls the shadows, shams, obliquities.   800

The streams of air that throng his timeless sky
Toss the green tree-tops, and not even sigh
In the slim nid-nod grass that seeds near by,
Or rob by a note the blackbird's lullaby.
And when the day breathes cold, and winds
     are high,   805
To watch the autumnal jackdaws storm the sky! –
Meal-dusty polls, glossed plumage, speedwell eye –
Ere cold of winter come; and Spring draw nigh.

And though the beauty both of bird and song
May pass unheeded in the press and throng,   810
In its own small for-ever it lived long.

Not by mere age, renown, power, place, or pride
The heart makes measurement. Its quickening
     tide
Found once its egress in a wounded side:

*'. . . When yet I had
not walkt above
A mile or two, from
my first love . . .'*

282

Love is its joyful citadel. Its moat   815
A lake of lilies, though they wither not.
Beyond our plummet's reach lies where they float.

Yet may we sound that deep as best we can,
And, unlike dazed Narcissus, there may scan   820
Reflections of the inestimable in man:

All that of truth is in its mirror shown;
And, far beneath, the ooze life feeds upon,
Whose *rot* breeds evil, jealousy and scorn.
A nature merciless, a mind forsworn.   825

from *Winged Chariot* (1951)

The title of *Winged Chariot* alludes to Andrew Marvell's poem 'To His Coy Mistress': 'But at my back I always hear/ Time's wingèd Chariot hurrying near'.[1] The allusion would suggest that the word '*Winged*' should have two syllables, as in the Marvell, but the Walter de la Mare enthusiasts I have talked to pronounce it with one. Whether or not this reflects de la Mare's own practice, I don't know.

Winged Chariot was first submitted to the publishers with the subtitle 'A Rambling Meditation on Time'. There is more structure to the poem than there first seems, but the original subtitle does give a good indication of what sort of poem *Winged Chariot* is. Unlike de la Mare's lyrics, and unlike the book-length allegorical narrative *The Traveller* (1945), *Winged Chariot* displays the qualities of de la Mare the anthologist and conversationalist, appearing to wander off the point while usually subtly augmenting it with by-the-ways and prompted reflections. It also makes space for the up-to-date and everyday and for proper nouns: this is a poem which mentions such figures as Karl Marx and such events as the discovery of the atom. The poem will modulate into a higher, more poetical register, but it starts in the world of Yale locks, daily routine and the speaking clock.

There is an argument for including the whole of *Winged Chariot* in this selection, not least as an example of how a poet can reinvent his style in old age. Moreover, as the work is not intended to be read as a chain of lyrics but as something more disquisitional, it is somewhat misleading to reproduce it in snippets. Nevertheless, to include all of a volume-length poem, as Auden did in his *A Choice of de la Mare's Verse*, would hugely unbalance this book in favour of one work. I have therefore reproduced the beginning of the poem to give readers its flavour, as well as two lyrical passages which read well as stand-alone poems. Lines are numbered according to where they fall in the complete, 1951 text of the poem.

Winged Chariot is written chiefly in rhymed tercets, though these are sometimes expanded to four or more lines employing same rhyme, and in iambic pentameter. Since the opening epigraph is, apart from the fragmented ending, also in this form of a rhymed tercet, I presume it is written by de la Mare himself.

'*I whom thou seest with horyloge . . .*', Sir Thomas More. According to William Roper, as a young man More devised 'in his father's house in London, a goodly hanging of fyne paynted cloth, with nyne pageauntes' [pageants]. In the seventh pageant was the image of Time, standing over that of Fame, who was in the pageant before. The verse which accompanied it reads in full:

> I whom thou seest with horyloge in hande,
> Am named Tyme, the lord of every howre.
> I shall in space destroy both see and lande.
> O simple Fame, how darest thou man honowre,
> Promising of his name, an endlesse flowre
> Who may in the world have a name eternall,
> When I shall in proces distroy the world and all.[2]

The quotation is presumably at the top of the poem in order to point out the futility of any authorial pursuit of fame in the face of time. A horyloge [horologue] is a timepiece or clock.

Throughout the poem, unidentified quotations are placed in the margins as a sort of commentary on the main text of the poem. Though it obviously has forerunners in marginalia, it is an exceptionally innovative juxtapositioning of poetic text and quotation.

l. 9 '*Three* emulous metal tongues you wake from sleep'. The hour, minute and second hands of a clock.

l. 12 'you search each face'. You scan the faces of the clocks.

l. 15 'you ring up *TIM*'. TIM became the nickname of the speaking clock because the numbers used to dial it – 846 – spelled out T, I, M. The much-used service started in 1936. TIM's voice at this time was that of London telephonist Ethel Jane Cain.[3]

l. 28 'O it came ore my eare . . .', Orsino's speech beginning 'If music be the food of love . . .', William Shakespeare, *Twelfth Night*, Act I, Sc. 1.

ll. 30–31. A 'Naiad' (l. 30), the name deriving from the Greek for 'to flow', is a water nymph, and here is the inhabitant of the 'river' of time. Time is often figured as a river or, in this case, a stream; the temporary stoppage or checking of time is usually figured as a stillness. To stop a river would, when it first happens at least, cause a turbulence, shattering the mirror of its surface, the 'imaged other-world' (l. 31) – the naiad here seeming to be a changed reflection of the person above.

ll. 34–5. The sound of the weir, which is so evocative in other poems and writings (see the notes to 'The Old Summerhouse' and 'Dreamland') and so hard to pin down, here has its meaning fixed, at least in relation to 'time's stream', as 'Eternity'. The mention of the weir may well also explain the quotation from *Twelfth Night*, for the line before it is 'That strain again, it had a dying fall', the dying fall perhaps being the sound of the weir (another reminder of 'The Old Summerhouse').

l. 43. 'Jack-go-to-bed-at-noon'. A yellow flower which looks a little like a dandelion and a lot like viper's grass; it only flowers in the morning sunshine and doesn't usually flower before June. Since Jack was the name de la Mare was known by, this may be a joke at himself.

l. 45. '. . . *Jocund day stands tiptoe on the mistie mountaine's top* . . .', William Shakespeare, *Romeo and Juliet*, Act III, Sc. 5. Romeo is responding to Juliet's insistence that they have heard a nightingale, making clear that it is a lark proclaiming morning; their night is over.

l. 45. 'Nimbused': surrounded by cloudy radiance in the manner of a deity.

l. 51. 'wheel and barrel, ratchet, pawl, and spring?' The winding mechanism of a clockwork watch. The spring is the source of energy; its winding mechanism has a ratchet attached with a pawl, which prevents the spring unwinding. The spring is enclosed inside a cylindrical box called the barrel; the main-spring turns the wheels.

l. 220. 'The shingled beach that I was Crusoe of'. Throughout de la Mare's life, Daniel Defoe's *Robinson Crusoe* was one of his favourite books; his book *Desert Islands* (1930) is a meditation upon it. As a very small child, while the family had money to do so, de la Mare holidayed on the Isle of Wight at Ventnor and Bonchurch.[4] Since Bonchurch beach is shingly, the memory is probably of there.

l. 127 '. . .*Those steps of stone* . . .' De la Mare may also be alluding to somewhere else, but, as Joe Griffiths notes, the tag is similar to a line in 'John Mouldy' and is identical to words in the passage of poetry next to it.[5]

l. 234. 'The waters of a reservoir'. This boyhood remembrance is, given the theme of the poem, interpretable as de la Mare's own childhood reaction to time. In addition to depicting time in terms of rivers and weirs, de la Mare would also figure the waters of time in terms of reservoirs. In his story 'The Vats', which arose from discussions about time with Edward Thomas, de la Mare describes coming upon the place where time is stored:

> I have called them the Vats. Vats they were not; but rather sunken Reservoirs; vast semi-spherical primeval Cisterns, of an area many times that of the bloated and swollen gasometers which float like huge flattened bubbles between earth and heaven under the sunlit clouds of the Thames.[6]

Having seen them, the narrator and his friend know 'now and forever that Time-pure *is*'.

l. 795 '. . . *When yet I had not walkt above / A mile or two from my first love . . .* , from 'The Retreat' by the metaphysical poet Henry Vaughan (1621–95). Vaughan is writing of his infancy. His 'first love' is God. The passage of *Winged Chariot* that accompanies this quotation may seem reminiscent of Wordsworth, especially the 'Ode: Intimations of Immortality', but it is Vaughan de la Mare has flanking his own text and presumably has in mind when he writes. The poem continues:

> And looking back – at that short space –
> Could see a glimpse of His bright face;
> When on some gilded cloud, or flow'r,
> My gazing soul would dwell an hour,
> And in those weaker glories spy
> Some shadows of eternity;[7]

l. 795. 'Better than that'. De la Mare has just asked the question:

> Would you rather your cranium of clockwork were?
> Its mainspring cleverness, its parts all 'spare';
> Its key mere habit, yet each tick, *Beware!*?

l. 797. '*Angelus*'. The *Angelus* is a Roman Catholic devotional prayer praising Mary and the Incarnation; it is also used in Anglican worship. The *Angelus* bell calls the devoted to prayer; de la Mare is contrasting it with the Angelus clock, an alarm clock.

l. 807. 'Meal-dusty polls': heads that look as if they were dusty with grain. Jackdaws have eyes of a similar blue to the flower of the 'speedwell'.

l. 817. 'Beyond our plummet's lead'. A plummet is a plumb line, a line with a lead weight at its bottom used to measure height or depth.

l. 819. 'Narcissus'. According to Greek mythology, Narcissus fell in love with his own reflection and, after taking his own life or simply withering away, was transformed into a flower.

l. 823. 'Whose *rot* breeds evil, jealousy and scorn'. De la Mare may well have in mind Shakespeare's Sonnet 94, with its closing line, 'Lilies that fester smell far worse than weeds', but both Shakespeare and de la Mare are indicating a natural phenomenon: rotting lilies are foul-smelling.

De Profundis

The metallic weight of iron;
The glaze of glass;
The inflammability of wood . . .

You will not be cold there;
You will not wish to see your face in a mirror;   5
There will be no heaviness,
Since you will not be able to lift a finger.

There will be company, but they will not heed you;
Yours will be a journey only of two paces
Into view of the stars again; but you will not make it.   10

There will be no recognition;
No one, who should see you, will say –
Throughout the uncountable hours –

'Why . . . the last time we met, I brought you some flowers!'

from *O Lovely England and Other Poems* (1953)

The title of 'De Profundis' derives from the Latin of Psalm 130: 'De profundis clamavi ad te, Domine'. In the King James Version, it reads: 'Out of the depths have I cried unto thee, O LORD'. The sonnet is not a cry to God, but an address to the reader, and perhaps to the poet himself, from 'two paces' (l. 9) below the ground, the depth at which a body is usually buried.

The poem's opening is deliberately disorientating, and the topic of the poem is at first a slight puzzle. Once the theme of mortality has been grasped, the items described in the first three lines may appear to refer to the constituents of a coffin – perhaps a glass-windowed casket with iron, as opposed to brass, handles – as it goes into the furnace of a crematorium. However, it seems more likely they are governed by the 'you' of the second stanza and refer to the condition of a corpse: corpses are a 'dead weight'; at death the eyes glaze (l. 2) over, a sight that haunts de la Mare's poems (see 'Good-Bye' and 'Dry August Burned'); they are also combustible.

The second stanza delineates the 'comforts' of the grave: its lack of cold (l. 4) and lack of need for vanity (l. 5) or feeling of 'heaviness' (l. 6). It is nearly that state of luxury in which, by convention, one does not have 'to lift a finger' (l. 7), but it is a state in which one is not able to lift a finger, or indeed to move at all. The 'company' which 'will not heed you' (l. 8) is the company of others buried in the graveyard. The journey of 'two paces' (l. 9) is not the burial but the journey out which 'you will not make' (l. 10).

The word 'recognition' (l. 11) is used both in the usual sense – you won't be able to recognise anything; you will also be unrecognisable – and in the sense that there will be no re-cognition: you will not be able to think again.

The last line is a half-joke and bears a strong similarity to a *bon mot* de la Mare made nearly a quarter of a century before, as recorded by John Bailey on 3 April 1928:

> Bruce Richmond has just told me a lovely story about Walter de la Mare. He is at last getting well fast after his very long illness, but he was for three weeks at the very gates of death. On one of these days his younger daughter said to him as she left him, 'Is there nothing I could get for you, fruit or flowers?' On which in a weak voice he could just – so characteristically – answer: 'No, no, my dear, too late for fruit, too soon for flowers!'[1]

Though de la Mare was evidently much preoccupied by death, there is little fear of it in his work. 'De Profundis' may be bleak in some ways, but it is quite prepared to look death in the face.

The moment Walter de la Mare so often wrote of and wondered about so much did not happen until 1956. Fittingly for a poet who loved the lengthening of the year's sunlight hours and the flowers of spring and who so captured the melancholy of their shortening, he died in the early hours of 22 June, the end of midsummer night.

Notes

INTRODUCTION (1)

1. See I. A. Richards, *Poetries and Sciences: A Reissue of Science and Poetry* (London: Routledge & Kegan Paul, 1926, 1935 and 1970), pp. 69–70 and F. R. Leavis, *New Bearings in English Poetry: A Study of the Contemporary Situation* (London: Chatto and Windus, 1950), pp. 50–1.
2. I. A. Richards 'Reconsideration: Walter de la Mare', *The New Republic*, vol. 174, No. 5, 31 Jan 1976, pp. 31–3: 33.
3. Ibid., p. 32.
4. Eric Linn Ormsby, *Fine Incisions: Essays on Poetry and Place* (Erin, Ontario: The Porcupine's Quill, 2011), p. 42.
5. *The Letters of T. S. Eliot, Volume 6: 1932–3*, edited by Valerie Eliot and Hugh Haffenden (London: Faber and Faber, 2016), p. 57.
6. Ibid.

JOHN MOULDY (15)

1. The biographical facts in this paragraph are derived from Theresa Whistler's *The Life of Walter de la Mare: Imagination of the Heart* (London: Duckworth, 1993).
2. *Animal Stories: Chosen, Arranged and in Some Part Rewritten* by Walter de la Mare (London: Faber and Faber, 1939), pp. xxi–xxii.
3. See Theresa Whistler, *The Life of Walter de la Mare*, p. 132.
4. Walter de la Mare, *Early One Morning in the Spring* (London: Faber and Faber, 1935), pp. 290–1.
5. 'On the Psychology of the Uncanny' (1906): Ernst Jentsch, translated by Roy Sellars in *Uncanny Modernity: Cultural Theories, Modern Anxieties*, edited by Jo Collins and John Jervis (Basingstoke: Palgrave Macmillan, 2008), pp. 216–28: p. 224.

6. See Peter Howarth, *British Poetry in the Age of Modernism* (Cambridge: Cambridge University Press, 2005), pp. 122–8.
7. https://en.wikipedia.org/wiki/Brown_rat.

THE FUNERAL (21)

1. Walter de la Mare, *Early One Morning in the Spring*, pp. 293–4.
2. These facts are derived from Theresa Whistler's *The Life of Walter de la Mare*.

AUTUMN (27)

1. Martha Bremser, 'The Voice of Solitude: the Children's Verse of Walter de la Mare', *Children's Literature*, vol. 21, 1993, pp. 66–91: p. 77.
2. Thomas Traherne, *The Poetical Works of Thomas Traherne*, edited by Glady I. Wade (London: P. J. & A. E. Dobell, 1932), p. 181.
3. Ibid., p. 183.
4. To my ears, the metre rests on two principal stresses in all its lines. These help the poem enact its rhythm of loss: each time the cadence of the line either rises ('There is a *wind*') or rests on a pitch ('Sad *wind*'), where 'sad' is a strong secondary stress, stating and underscoring present coldnesses and absences. This is counterbalanced by how the end of the line falls away ('*rose* was', '*grass* was') underscoring the passing away of what had once been there. But others may choose to count 'sad' or 'was' as metre-bearing stresses.
5. Horace Gregory, 'The Nocturnal Traveller: Walter de la Mare', in *The Dying Gladiators and Other Essays* (New York: Grove Press; London Evergreen Books: 1961), pp. 63–78: p. 73.

THE BIRTHNIGHT: TO F. (31)

1. John Bayley, 'No Full Stop: the movement of Golding's fiction', from the publication accompanying the British Council exhibition entitled 'William Golding 1911–93', 1994. At the time of writing, the article was freely available at: www.walterdelamare.co.uk/25.html.
2. Ibid.

3. Eric Ormsby, *Fine Incisions: Essays on Poetry and Place*, p. 43.
4. All the biographical details here derive from Theresa Whistler, *The Life of Walter de la Mare*. The diary is quoted on p. 90.

NAPOLEON (35)

1. Adam Zamoyski, *1812: Napoleon's Fatal March on Moscow* (London: Harper Perennial, 2005), p. 536.
2. Ibid.
3. A. P. Wavell, *Other Men's Flowers*, memorial edition (London: Jonathan Cape, 1952), p. 95.
4. *The French Revolution and Napoleon: a Sourcebook*, edited by Philip G. Dwyer and Peter McPhee (London: Routledge, 2002), p. 184.
5. *Metternich's Europe: Selected Documents*, edited by Mack Walker (London: Palgrave Macmillan, 1968), p. 27.
6. Ibid., p. 29.
7. Walter de la Mare, *Come Hither: a Collection of Rhymes and Poems for the Young of All Ages*, illustrated by Diana Bloomfield (Harmondsworth: Puffin and Longman, 1973), vol. 1, pp. 422–3.
8. Ibid, p. 423.
9. Walter de la Mare, *Desert Islands*, with decorations by Rex Whistler (London: Faber and Faber, 1930), pp. 205–6.
10. See Joe Griffiths, 'The Changing World of Walter de la Mare's Poetry', *The Walter de la Mare Society Journal*, no. 10, January 2007, pp. 38–48: p. 47.

LONGLEGS (41)

1. Walter de la Mare, *Come Hither*, vol. 1, p. 365.
2. Walter de la Mare, *Down-Adown-Derry: A Book of Fairy Poems* (London: Constable, 1922), p. 112.
3. Helen Thomas, *As It Was* and *World Without End* (London: Faber and Faber, 1972), p. 119.
4. Edward Thomas, review of Walter de la Mare, *Poems*, in the *Daily Chronicle*, 9 November 1906, in Edward Thomas, *A Language Not to be Betrayed: Selected Poems of Edward Thomas*, selected, with

an introduction by Edna Longley (Manchester: Carcanet, 1981), pp. 97–8: p. 97.

5. Edward Thomas, *Collected Poems*, with a foreword by Walter de la Mare (London: Selwyn and Blount, 1920), p. xii.

6. Ibid.

7. For a sketch of Thomas and de la Mare's circle in St George's Yard, see Matthew Hollis, *Now All Roads Lead to France: the Last Years of Edward Thomas* (London: Faber and Faber, 2011), p. 93.

8. Eleanor Farjeon, *Edward Thomas: The Last Four Years* (London: Oxford University Press, 1958), p. 36.

9. *Edward Thomas's Poets*, edited by Judy Kendall (Manchester, Carcanet, 2007), p. 133.

10. Helen Thomas, undated letter to Walter de la Mare, Walter de la Mare Archive, Bodleian Library, Box 132.

11. Edward Thomas, *Light and Twilight* (London: Duckworth, 1911), p. 47.

12. On 24 April 1910, Thomas writes of de la Mare coming down that Friday (which would have been 29 April). He signs himself 'Longlegs' in a letter postmarked 8 May. *Poet to Poet: Edward Thomas's Letters to Walter de la Mare*, edited by Judy Kendall, transcriber's preface by Piers Pennington (Bridgend: Seren, 2012), pp. 76–8.

13. Helen Thomas, *As It Was* and *World Without End*, p. 133.

14. Edward Thomas, *In Pursuit of Spring* (London, Edinburgh, Dublin and New York: Thomas Nelson and Sons, 1914), pp. 175–6.

15. Angela Leighton, *Hearing Things: The Work of Sound in Literature* (Cambridge Mass.: Belknap Press, 2018), p. 134.

KING DAVID (47)

1. Jeremy Dibble, 'Hidden Artifice: Howells as Songwriter' in *The Music of Herbert Howells*, edited by Philip A. Cooke and David Maw (Woodbridge: The Boydell Press, 2013), pp. 62–85: p. 80.

2. Farid ud-din Attar, *The Conference of the Birds*, translated by Afham Darbandi and Dick Davis (London: Penguin, 1984).

3. Edward Thomas to Walter de la Mare, letter, 8 June 1909, *Poet to Poet: Edward Thomas's Letters to Walter de la Mare*, p. 65.

4. That same year Thomas set down his own experience of nightingale song in *The South Country* (London: J. M. Dent, 1932; originally published 1909), pp. 35–6.

5. It may be in response to Thomas's objection that in the 1944 edition of *Collected Rhymes and Verses*, de la Mare altered the word 'ease' (l. 4) to 'solace', thus sacrificing some of the music of the original (the word makes an internal consonance with 'cause' (l. 2) and an internal assonance with the repeated 'he' (l. 2 and l. 3) and 'melancholy' (l .4)). This change makes its way into the revised (1974) edition of the 1969 *Complete Poems*, which is the text usually followed by this edition. But since de la Mare sanctioned 'ease' for publication in the Edward Ardizonne-illustrated 1945 edition of *Peacock Pie*, which remains in print, I feel justified in deviating from my usual practice of following the revised *Complete Poems* and have kept the poem's original wording.

6. Christopher Palmer, *Herbert Howells: A Study* (Seven Oaks: Novell, 1978), p. 16.

7. I am following, and in part repeating, the account of the setting by Christopher Palmer, ibid., pp. 41–2.

8. Paul Spicer, 'Howells' Use of the Melisma: Word Setting in His Songs and Choral Music', in *The Music of Herbert Howells* , edited by Philip A. Cooke and David Maw (Woodbridge: The Boydell Press, 2013), pp. 100–117: p. 102.

9. Richard Stokes, The *Penguin Book of English Song: Seven Centuries of Poetry from Chaucer to Auden* (London: Penguin Classics, 2016), p. 742, on the authority of Brian N. S. Gooch and David S. Thacker, *Musical Settings of Late Victorian and Modern British Literature: A Catalogue* (New York: Garland, 1976).

10. Colin Scott-Sutherland, 'Song of the Water Midden', *Walter de la Mare Society Magazine*, Nov. 2010, pp. 33–46: p. 34.

11. Adèle L. Paxton, *Solo Song Settings of the Poetry of Walter de la Mare: A Bibliography* (London: Walter de la Mare Society, 2011).

AN EPITAPH (53)

1. Edward Thomas, letter to Walter de la Mare, 14 June 1908, *Poet to Poet: Edward Thomas's Letters to Walter de la Mare*, p. 44. For the

detail about the cake box, see Russell Brain, *Tea with Walter de La Mare* (London: Faber and Faber, 1957), p. 34.

2. Quoted in Theresa Whistler, *The Life of Walter de la Mare*, p. 210.

3. Ibid., pp. 179–80.

4. See Jill Benton, *Avenging Muse: Naomi Royde-Smith, 1875–1964* (Bloomington, Indiana: Xlibris, 2015), p. 153.

THE BELLS (61)

1. William Wordsworth, *Poetical Works*, edited by Thomas Hutchinson, revised by Ernest de Selincourt (Oxford & New York: Oxford University Press, 1969), p. 149.

2. Ibid., p. 230.

3. Geoffrey H. Hartman, *Wordsworth's Poetry 1787–1814* (New Haven and London: Yale University Press, 1964), p. 269.

4. Walter de la Mare, *Out of the Deep* (London: British Library, 2017), p. 169.

THE LISTENERS (67)

1. Michael Rosen, 'What is a Bong Tree?' Lecture for Centre for Literacy in Primary Education official event, September 2007, https://www.michaelrosen.co.uk/writings-on-poetry/.

2. Boris Ford, 'The Rest was Silence', *Encounter*, 36, September 1956, pp. 38–46.

3. Anne Bentinck, 'Personal Interview with Mr Richard de la Mare at Much Hadham Hall, 25 July 1979', *Walter de la Mare Society Magazine,* November 2001.

4. F. L. Lucas, *The Decline and Fall of the Romantic Ideal* (Cambridge: Cambridge University Press, 1948), p. 22.

5. Walter de la Mare, letter to J. G. Syme, 7 February 1944, as quoted in Whistler, *The Life of Walter de la Mare*, p. 203.

6. Walter de la Mare Archive, Bodleian Library, Oxford, Box A55.

7. The remark was made to Laurence Whistler in 1951 and is quoted by Theresa Whistler, *The Life of Walter de la Mare*, p. 401.

8. Walter de la Mare, handwritten annotation to T. R. Henn, *The Apple and the Spectroscope*, foreword by Lawrence Bragg (London: Methuen, 1951), p. 42. Walter de la Mare Library, Senate House, University College, London.

9. Quoted in Theresa Whistler, unedited typescript of *The Life of Walter de la Mare*, Walter de la Mare archive, Bodleian Library, Oxford.

10. Arthur Symons, *The Symbolist Movement in Literature* (London: Constable, 1911), p. 135.

11. Giles de la Mare, 'Exploring the World of Walter de la Mare's "The Listeners"', *Walter de la Mare Society Magazine*, 13 June 2010, pp. 9–17.

12. Angela Leighton, *Hearing Things: The Work of Sound in Literature* (Cambridge, Mass.: Belknap Press, 2018), p. 140.

13. *Short Stories 1895–1926*, edited by Giles de la Mare (London: Giles de la Mare Publishers, 1996), p. 81.

14. Ibid., p. 82.

15. Ibid., p. 83.

16. Theresa Whistler, *The Life of Walter de la Mare*, p. 303.

17. Walter de la Mare, *Come Hither*, vol. 1, p. 12.

18. Ibid., p. 22.

19. Letter to C. L. Young, 7 December 1917, quoted in Lawrance Thompson, *Robert Frost: The Years of Triumph, 1915–38* (New York: Holt, Rinehart and Winston, 1970), p. 118.

20. Peter Howarth, *British Poetry in the Age of Modernism* (Cambridge: Cambridge University Press, 2006), p. 127.

21. Ibid.

22. Derek Attridge, 'In Defence of the Dolnik: Twentieth-Century British Verse in Free Four-Beat Metre', *Études Britanniques Contemporaines*, 39, 2010, pp. 5–18.

23. Walter de la Mare reciting 'The Listeners', British Library audio file, 1CDR0003832.BD18.mp3.

24. Walter de la Mare, *Come Hither*, vol. 1, p. 318.

25. Ibid., pp. 318–19.

26. Ibid., p. 320.

THE KEYS OF MORNING (91)

1. Quoted in Theresa Whistler, *The Life of Walter de la Mare*, p. 416.
2. Walter de la Mare, *Behold, This Dreamer!* (London: Faber and Faber, 1984), p. 57.
3. Forrest Reid, *Walter de la Mare: A Critical Study* (London: Faber and Faber, 1939), p. 154.

THE PIGS AND THE CHARCOAL BURNER (97)

1. Walter de la Mare, *Out of the Deep*, p. 253.
2. See Joseph Orefice, 'Pigs 'n Trees', Cornell Small Farms Program, Cornell University website, http://smallfarms.cornell.edu/2016/01/11/pigs-n-trees/.
3. Henry Charles Duffin, *Walter de la Mare: a Study of his Poetry* (New York: Haskell House, 1970), p. 87.

ALL THAT'S PAST (101)

1. F. R. Leavis, *New Bearings in English Poetry: A Study of the Contemporary Situation* (London: Chatto and Windus, 1950), p. 51.
2. Robert Graves, *Goodbye to All That* (Harmondsworth: Penguin, 1973), p. 256.
3. Paul Edwards, 'British War Memoirs' in *The Cambridge Companion to the Literature of the First World War*, edited by Vincent Sherry (Cambridge: Cambridge University Press, 2005), electronic edition.
4. Theresa Whistler, *The Life of Walter de la Mare*, p. 158.
5. Walter de la Mare to Ella Coltman, 20 May 1909, quoted in Theresa Whistler, *The Life of Walter de la Mare*, p. 158.
6. Typescript and proofs of *The Listeners*, Walter de la Mare Archive, Bodleian Library, Oxford, Box A55.

"THE HAWTHORN HATH A DEATHLY SMELL" (107)

1. D. C. Watts, *Elsevier's Dictionary of Plant Lore* (Burlington, San Diego and London: Elsevier, 2007), p. 182.

2. *Poems of Henry Vaughan, Silurist*, vol. 1, edited by E. K. Chambers, introduction by H. C. Beeching (London: Lawrence and Bullen, 1896), p. 267.
3. Margaret Baker, *Discovering the Folklore of Plants* (London: Shire Books, 1992), p. 97.
4. Ibid., pp. 104 and 383.
5. William Blake, *Blake's Poetry and Designs*, edited by Mary Lynn Johnson and John E. Grant (New York and London: W. W. Norton, 1979), p. 289.
6. See Susan S. Eberly, 'A Thorn among the Lilies: The Hawthorn in Medieval Love Allegory', *Folklore*, 1 January 1989, vol. 100 (1), pp. 41–52.
7. Quoted in Theresa Whistler, *The Life of Walter de la Mare*, p. 181.

A SONG OF ENCHANTMENT (113)

1. Chris Howkins, *The Elder: The Mother Tree of Folklore* (Addlestone, Surrey: C. Howkins, 1996), p. 27.
2. For instance, the dedication to one of de la Mare's favourite books, Robert Herrick's *Hesperides*, contains the lines 'But when that men have both well drunke, and fed,/ Let my enchantments then be sung', Robert Herrick, *Hesperides or the Works Humane and Divine* (London: William Pickering, 1846), p. 4.

THE BEES' SONG (117)

1. See Leonard Clark, *Walter de la Mare* (London: The Bodley Head, 1960), p. 22.
2. See Jill Benton, *Avenging Muse: Naomi Royde-Smith, 1875–1964*, pp. 165–6 and p. 193. The figuring of writing as honey turns up in Naomi Royde-Smith's novel *John Fanning's Legacy* (London: Constable, 1927), which was, though he didn't take credit for it, co-written with de la Mare: 'People are so silly about the uses of life. Nobody blames the bee because it makes honey from flower-juices instead of buzzing sermons about the fruit', pp. 175–6. In her late novel *Melilot* (London: Robert Hale, 1955), it is extolled by von Airth, a character clearly based on de la Mare. Melilot,

the heroine, is named after a flower associated with bees and the making of honey.

3. https://en.wikipedia.org/wiki/Zayin.

THE HONEY ROBBERS (123)

1. I thank Jane Wright for pointing this out to me.
2. I thank Kyra Larkin for telling me about dreidels. Further details from https://www.myjewishlearning.com/article/how-to-play-dreidel/.
3. Maurice Maeterlinck, *The Life of the Bee* (London: Ballantyne, Hanson & Co., 1901), pp. 45–6.

THE MOCKING FAIRY (129)

1. See Cassandra Eason, *A Complete Guide to Fairies and Magical Beings* (San Francisco and Newburyport: Weiser Books, 2001), p. 164.
2. See Theresa Whistler, *The Life of Walter de la Mare*, p. 212.
3. Katherine Mansfield, *Poems of Katherine Mansfield* (Auckland, Oxford, Melbourne: Oxford University Press, 1988), p. 64.
4. See Theresa Whislter, *The Life of Walter de la Mare*, pp. 213–14.

THE SONG OF THE MAD PRINCE (133)

1. *Bells and Grass: A Book of Rhymes* by Walter de la Mare with illustrations by J. Rowland Emett (London: Faber and Faber, 1941), p. 8.
2. I. A. Richards, *Poetries and Sciences: A Reissue of Science and Poetry* (London: Routledge & Kegan Paul, 1926, 1935 and 1970), p. 69.
3. Filomena Aguiar de Vasconcelos, 'The Song of the Mad Prince: The Me that Sings Throughout' (Porto: Universidade do Porto. Faculdade de Letras, 2001). The article is available at ler.letras. up.pt/uploads/ficheiros/artigo612.pdf and is adapted from her doctoral dissertation 'That's What I Said'. Dimensões do Sujeito na Poesia de Walter de Ia Maré. (FLUP, 1995).

4. Thomas Hardy, *The Collected Letters of Thomas Hardy*, edited by Richard Little Purdy and Michael Millgate, vol. 5 (Oxford: Clarendon Press, 1985), p. 330.

FOR ALL THE GRIEF (141)

1. See Jill Benton, *Avenging Muse: Naomi Royde-Smith, 1875–1964*, p. 170.
2. In Brooke's letter of Friday, 20 November, he talks of having seen de la Mare on Thursday, which was 19 November: Rupert Brooke, Letter to Walter de la Mare, 20 November 1914, Imperial War Museum, Document 10436.
3. *The Collected Poems of Rupert Brooke, with a Memoir by Sir Edward Marsh* (London: Sidgwick & Jackson, 1930), p. cxvi.
4. Ibid., p. cxxxi.
5. See Christopher Hassall, *Rupert Brooke: A Biography* (London: Faber and Faber, 1972), p. 472.
6. Walter de la Mare, 'Happy England', *Times Literary Supplement*, 27 August 1914.
7. *The Collected Poems of Rupert Brooke*, p. 144.
8. Ibid.

FARE WELL (145)

1. Theresa Whistler, *The Life of Walter de la Mare*, p. 284.
2. Walter de la Mare, 'Thoughts by England Given', anonymous review of *New Numbers*, vol. 4, *Times Literary Supplement*, 11 March 1915.
3. *The Collected Poems of Rupert Brooke*, p. 148.
4. See William Wootten, 'A Richer Dust – Afterlives of Rupert Brooke', *Times Literary Supplement*, 24 April 2015, pp. 13–15.
5. Quoted by Sean Street, *The Dymock Poets* (Bridgend: Seren, 1994), p. 133.
6. See Naomi Royde-Smith, *Avenging Muse*, p. 174.
7. Derek Walcott interviewed by Sue Lawley, *Desert Island Discs*, BBC Radio, first broadcast 15 November 1992, www.bbc.co.uk/programmes/p0093z3h.

8. Theresa Whistler, *The Life of Walter de la Mare*, p. 446.

9. John Bayley, *Housman's Poems* (Oxford: Clarendon Press, 1992), p. 175.

10. The relationship between Sonnet 106 and 'Fare Well' was pointed out to me by Giles de la Mare.

11. Theresa Whistler, *The Life of Walter de la Mare*, p. 324.

12. *Marcus Manilius Astronomicon* (London: Richards Grant, 1930), pp. xxv–xxxvi.

13. John Bayley, *Housman's Poems*, pp. 172–5.

THE SCRIBE (155)

1. William Blake, *Blake's Poetry and Designs*, p. 209.

2. Lingard, John, "'The Verge at Which They Fail": Language, Relationship, and Journey in the Poetry of Walter de la Mare', *Dalhousie Review*, 69 (4), 1989/90, 57893, p. 582.

3. William Blake, *Blake's Poetry and Designs*, p. 19.

TO E.T.: 1917 (159)

1. Walter de la Mare, undated letter to Edward Thomas (probably written in the spring of 1915), Edward Garnett Papers, Harry Ransom Centre, Texas.

2. Walter de la Mare, *Private View*, introduction by Lord David Cecil (London: Faber and Faber, 1952), p. 116.

3. Jean Moorcroft Wilson, *Edward Thomas: From Adlestrop to Arras* (London: Bloomsbury, 2015), pp. 412–13.

4. See Thomas's letter to de la Mare postmarked 6 October 1913: 'Thank you for what you said last night. I think I have now changed my mind though I have the saviour in my pocket.' *Poet to Poet: Edward Thomas's Letters to Walter de la Mare*, edited by Judy Kendall, transcriber's preface by Piers Pennington (Bridgend: Seren, 2012), pp. 169–70.

5. Edward Thomas, *Collected Poems*, with a foreword by Walter de la Mare (London: Faber and Faber, 1979), p. 6.

6. Ibid. p. 12.

SOTTO VOCE (165)

1. Mark Constantine and the Sound Approach, *The Sound Approach to Birding: A Guide to Understanding Birdsound* (Poole: The Sound Approach, 2006), p. 95.
2. Christina Rossetti, *Poems and Prose*, edited with an introduction by Simon Humphries (Oxford: Oxford University Press, 2008), p. 108.
3. Walter de la Mare, *Come Hither*, vol. 1, p. 339.
4. John Keats, *Selected Poems*, edited by John Barnard (London: Penguin, 2007), p. 12.
5. Edward Thomas to Walter de la Mare, 24 March 1915 in *Poet to Poet: Edward Thomas's Letters to Walter de la Mare*, p. 201.
6. Walter de la Mare, 'Edward Thomas', first published in the *Times Literary Supplement*, 18 October, 1917; *Private View*, pp. 119–22: p. 119.
7. For a further elaboration of the themes raised here, see my essay '"A Richer" Opportunity: Walter de la Mare's Presentations of Edward Thomas', *Edward Thomas: Roads from Arras* (Manchester: Cambridge Scholars, 2018). The essay also points out the allusions to Rossetti and Keats.
8. *The Shakespeare Songs: Being a Complete Collection of the Songs written by or attributed to William Shakespeare*, edited by Tucker Brooke, introduction by Walter de la Mare (London: J. M. Dent, 1929), p. xxii.
9. Walter de la Mare, *A Choice of De La Mare's Verse*, edited by W. H. Auden (London: Faber and Faber, 1963).
10. Edward Thomas, *The Annotated Collected Poems*, edited by Edna Longley (Newcastle: Bloodaxe, 2008), p. 55.
11. Walter de la Mare, *Behold, This Dreamer!*, p. 263.

TITMOUSE (173)

1. Walter de la Mare, *Come Hither*, vol. 1, p. 409.
2. *Animal Stories: Chosen, Arranged and in Some Part Rewritten by* Walter de la Mare (London: Faber and Faber, 1939), pp. xlviii–xlix.

3. Cora Diamond, 'Eating Meat and Eating People', *Philosophy*, vol. 53, no. 206, October 1978), pp. 465–79. The essay is collected in Diamond's book *The Realistic Spirit: Wittgenstein, Philosophy, and the Mind* (Cambridge, Mass. and London: MIT Press, 1991).

4. Ibid., p. 474.

GOOD-BYE (177)

1. Forrest Reid to Walter de la Mare, 13 December 1921, Walter de la Mare Archive, Bodleian Library, Oxford, Box B107.

2. Forrest Reid to Walter de la Mare, 4 January 1922, Walter de la Mare Archive, Bodleian Library, Oxford, Box B107.

3. 'Poetry in Walter de la Mare', *The Denver Quarterly*, 8.3, Autumn 1973, pp. 69–81.

4. Eric Ormsby, *Fine Incisions: Essays on Poetry and Place* (Erin, Ontario: The Porcupine's Quill, 2011), p. 45.

5. See Elizabeth Bishop's 'Reviewed Work: *Come Hither: A Collection of Rhymes and Poems for the Young of All Ages* by Walter de la Mare', *Poetry*, vol. 93, no. 1, October 1958, pp. 50–4.

THE RAILWAY JUNCTION (181)

1. Graham Greene, 'The Short Stories', in *Tribute to Walter de la Mare on his Seventy-fifth Birthday* (London: Faber and Faber, 1948), pp. 71–7: p. 71.

2. James Reeves, *Understanding Poetry* (London: Heinemann, 1965), pp. 92–4.

TO K.M. (187)

1. Kathleen Jones, *Katherine Mansfield: The Story-Teller* (Edinburgh: Edinburgh University Press, 2010), p. 488.

2. Jenny McDonnell, '"Memorials of the Dead": Walter de la Mare, Katherine Mansfield, and the Literary Afterlife' in *Katherine Mansfield and the Bloomsbury Group*, edited by Todd Martin (London: Bloomsbury, 2017), ebook. McDonnell also establishes details of the poem's first publication.

3. De la Mare writes asking permission in his letter of 15 January 1922. It is clear from his letter that Mansfield had already seen the poem. Letter from Walter de la Mare to Katherine Mansfield, 15 January 1922, Newberry Library, Chicago, Katherine Mansfield Papers, Box 7.

4. See Jenny McDonnell, '"Memorials of the Dead": Walter de la Mare, Katharine Mansfield, and the Literary Afterlife'. De la Mare worked to place other stories by Mansfield.

5. Letter from Walter de la Mare to Katherine Mansfield, 15 January 1922, Newberry Library, Chicago, Katherine Mansfield Papers, Box 7.

6. J. Lawrence Mitchell tracks down the date and place of the meeting in 'Katherine Mansfield and "The Man Who Came to Tea"', *Journal of Modern Literature*, vol. 18, no. 1, Winter 1992, pp. 147–55: p. 149.

7. Katherine Mansfield, *The Katherine Mansfield Notebooks*, vol. 2, edited by Margaret Scott (Canterbury, New Zealand: Lincoln University Press, 1997), p. 312.

8. See Theresa Whistler, *The Life of Walter de la Mare*, p. 307.

9. Walter de la Mare, 'Prelude', review of *Bliss and Other Stories*, *Athenaeum*, 21 January 1921.

10. Ida Baker [writing as Leslie Moore], *Katherine Mansfield: The Memories of LM* (London: Michael Joseph, 1971), p. 197.

11. Theresa Whistler, *The Life of Walter de la Mare*, p. 306.

12. Walter de la Mare to Katherine Mansfield, 22 January 1921. For Mansfield's letter, see Theresa Whistler, *The Life of Walter de la Mare*, p. 306.

13. https://www.woodlandtrust.org.uk/visiting-woods/trees-woods-and-wildlife/british-trees/common-non-native-trees/cedar/.

14. J. Lawrence Mitchell, believing the poem to have been conceived as an elegy, mistakenly identifies this as the horse of death from Revelation 6:8, op. cit., p. 148.

15. Walter de la Mare, *Come Hither*, vol. 1, p. 158.

16. Ibid, p. 160.

17. http://faeryfolklorist.blogspot.co.uk/2011/06/thomas-rhymer-melrose.html.

18. Katherine Mansfield, letter to John Middleton Murry, 12 October 1920, *The Collected Letters of Katherine Mansfield*, vol. 4, ed. Vincent Sullivan and Margaret Scott (Oxford: Clarendon Press, 1996), p. 67.
19. The details of the first publishing of the poem in the *Saturday Westminster Gazette* are noted by Jenny McDonnell in '"Memorials of the Dead": Walter de la Mare, Katherine Mansfield and the Literary Afterlife' in *Katherine Mansfield and the Bloomsbury Group*.
20. Walter de la Mare, *Come Hither*, vol. 2, p. 772.

THE FECKLESS DINNER-PARTY (197)

1. Typescripts for *The Veil*, Walter de la Mare Library, Bodleian Library, Oxford, Box A103.
2. See *Come Hither*, vol. 2, p. 880.
3. 'Meaning in Poetry', unpublished typescript of lecture, Walter de la Mare Archive, Bodleian Library, Oxford, Box A1178.
4. Lady Desborough's dinner parties are identified as the inspiration for 'The Feckless Dinner-Party' in Richard Davenport-Hines, *Ettie: The Intimate Life and Dauntless Spirit of Lady Desborough* (London: Weidenfeld and Nicolson, 2008), p. 268.

REFLECTIONS (205)

1. Walter de la Mare, 'Rupert Brooke and the Intellectual Imagination' in *Pleasures and Speculations* (London: Faber and Faber, 1940), pp. 172–99.
2. Ibid., pp. 179–80.
3. Sigmund Freud, 'The Theme of the Three Caskets', *The Standard Edition of the Complete Psychological Works of Sigmund Freud*, vol. 12 (1911–13): *The Case of Schreber, Papers on Technique and Other Works*, edited by James Strachey, (London: Vintage, 2001), pp. 289–302: 295.

ROSE (211)

1. Walter de la Mare, 'Thomas Campion', *Saturday Westminster Gazette*, 8 January 1910.

2. W. H. Auden cites Campion as a key influence on de la Mare in 'An Appreciation of the Lyric Verse of Walter de la Mare', *New York Times Book Review*, 26 February 1956.

3. Walter de la Mare, *Come Hither*, pp. 404–5.

4. John Bayley, 'The Unexpectedness of Walter de la Mare', *The Walter de la Mare Society Magazine*, July 2002, pp. 4–6: p. 4.

AWAY (215)

1. Alice Munro, *Too Much Happiness* (London: Vintage, 2010), pp. 138–63; Angela Leighton, *Hearing Things: The Work of Sound in Literature* (Cambridge Mass. and London: Belknap Press, 2018), pp. 148–51 and pp. 156–7.

2. Alice Munro, *Too Much Happiness*, p. 161.

THOMAS HARDY (219)

1. Thomas Hardy, letter to Walter de la Mare, 1 November 1918, *The Collected Letters of Thomas Hardy*, edited by Richard Littlepurdy and Michael Millgate, vol. 5 (Oxford: Clarendon Press, 1985), p. 284.

2. Theresa Whistler, *The Life of Walter de la Mare*, p. 311.

3. Walter de la Mare, 'Meeting Thomas Hardy', *The Listener*, 28 April 1955, pp. 756–7: p. 756.

4. Florence Emily Hardy, *The Life of Thomas Hardy 1840–1928* (London and Basingstoke: Macmillan, 1972), p. 442.

5. Ibid, p. 413.

6. See Theresa Whistler, *The Life of Walter de la Mare*, pp. 313–14. Whistler states that 'Thomas Hardy' also appeared in that issue of the *London Mercury*, but while de la Mare does have a poem in the issue, it is 'The Last Coachload', *London Mercury*, vol. 5. no. 26, pp. 119–23.

7. Most of Yui Kajita's work on Hardy and de la Mare has yet to be published at the time of writing. She has, however, been generous enough to share with me the essay '"Something Tapped": Haunting Echoes in Thomas Hardy and Walter de la Mare', which says far more about the subject than I can cover here.

8. Edward Thomas, *The Annotated Collected Poems*, p. 51.

DRY AUGUST BURNED (225)

1. Theresa Whistler, *The Life of Walter de la Mare*, p. 170.
2. Ibid., p. 367.
3. See, for instance, https://en.wikipedia.org/wiki/Stubble_burning.
4. Walter de la Mare, *Animal Stories*, p. 75.
5. Quoted in Marianne Taylor, *The Way of the Hare* (London: Bloomsbury, 2017), p. 32.

INCANTATION (231)

1. Walter de la Mare, *Come Hither*, vol. 1, p. 318.
2. *The Shakespeare Songs: Being a Complete Collection of the Songs written by or attributed to William Shakespeare*, p. xviii.
3. Charlotte de la Tour, *The Language of Flowers* (Philadelphia: Saunders and Otley, 1839), p. 34.
4. John Lingard also investigates the meaning of these words, with slightly different findings, in '"The Verge at which They Fail": Language, Relationship and Journey in the Poetry of Walter de la Mare', *Dalhousie Review*, 69 (4), 1989/90, pp. 578–93.
5. C. K. Ogden and I. A. Richards, *The Meaning of Meaning: a Study of the Influence of Language Upon Thought and of the Science of Symbolosm*, supplementary essays by B. Malinowski and F. G. Crookshank (London: Kegan Paul, Trench, Trubner & Co. Ltd, 1923; New York: Harcourt, Brace and Company Inc., 1923), p. 87. De la Mare refers to it in his lecture 'Meaning in Poetry', Walter de la Mare Archive, Bodleian Library, Oxford, Box A117.
6. Frits Staal, *Rules without Meaning: Ritual, Mantras and the Human Sciences* (New York: Peter Lang, 1990), p. 282.
7. Walter de la Mare, *Short Stories 1895–1926*, p. 82.
8. Walter de la Mare, *The Return*, p. 241.

BRUEGHEL'S WINTER (237)

1. Sir William Nicholson, Letter to Walter de la Mare 13 May 1936, Walter de la Mare Archive, Bodleian Library, Oxford, Box B97.

2. W. H. Auden, 'Jacob and the Angel', review of *Behold, This Dreamer!* by Walter de la Mare, *New Republic*, 27 December 1939; *The Complete Works of W. H. Auden: Prose*, vol. 2, *1939–48*, edited by Edward Mendelson (Princeton, New Jersey: Princeton University Press, 2002), pp. 37–9: p. 37.

3. W. H. Auden, *Making Knowing and Judging*, An Inaugural Lecture delivered before the University of Oxford on 11 June 1956 (Clarendon Press: Oxford, 1956).

THE OLD SUMMERHOUSE (247)

1. Walter de la Mare, *The Return*, p. 125.

2. Walter de la Mare, Letter to Naomi Royde-Smith, 1 April 1913, as quoted by Whistler, *The Life of Walter de la Mare*, p. 214.

3. Peter Scupham, 'Walter de la Mare', *PN Review*, 25 (6), July 1999, pp. 44–6: p. 44.

4. John Keats, *The Poetical Works of John Keats*, edited by Francis T. Palgrave (London: Macmillan, 1928), p. 215.

"OF A SON" (251)

1. These facts derive from https://en.wikipedia.org/wiki/Henri_Désiré_Landru, and 'Henri Landru: The Real-Life Bluebeard Murderer of France', http://www.medicalbag.com/grey-matter/henri-landru-the-real-life-bluebeard-murderer-of-france/article/472777/.

THE HOUSE (257)

1. See Edward Thomas, *The South Country*, introduction by Helen Thomas, illustrated by Eric Fitch Daglish (London: J. M Dent, 1932), pp. 57–9 and pp. 241–5.

2. Samuel Taylor Coleridge, *Biographia Literaria* (London: Rest Fenner, 1817), p. 296.

3. Quoted in Jill Benton, *Avenging Muse: Naomi Royde-Smith, 1875–1964* (Bloomington, Indiana: Xlibris, 2015), p. 153.

DREAMLAND (263)

1. Walter de la Mare, *Crossings: A Fairy Play with Music by C. Armstrong Gibbs* (London: W. Collins, 1923), p. 11.
2. Walter de la Mare, *Bells and Grass: A Book of Rhymes*, p. 7.

SALLIE (267)

1. Walter de la Mare, *Crossings*, p. 11.
2. Stephen Banfield, *Sensibility and English Song: Critical Studies of the Early 20th Century* (Cambridge, New York, Melbourne: Cambridge University Press, 1984), p. 226.

THE HOUSE (271)

1. In, for example, Charlotte de la Tour, *The Language of Flowers*, p. 136.
2. *Come Hither*, vol. 1, p. 302.
3. Edward Thomas, Letter to Walter de la Mare, 7 December 1907, *Poet to Poet: Edward Thomas's Letters to Walter de la Mare*, p. 31.
4. Matthew Hollis, *Now All Roads Lead to France*, p. 192.
5. Edward Thomas, *The Annotated Collected Poems*, p. 37.

WINGED CHARIOT (277)

1. Andrew Marvell, *Poems of Andrew Marvell*, edited by James Reeves and Martin Seymour-Smith (London: Heinemann, 1969), p. 33.
2. William Roper, *The Life of Sir Thomas More*, edited by S. W. Singer (London: C. Whittingham, 1822), p. 189.
3. https://www.speaking-clock.com.
4. See Whistler, *The Life of Walter de la Mare*, p. 13.
5. Joe Griffiths, 'The Marginal Quotations in *Winged Chariot*', *Walter de la Mare Society Magazine*, no. 6, February 2003, pp. 33–47: 38.
6. Walter de la Mare, *Short Stories 1895–1926*, edited by Giles de la Mare (London: Giles de la Mare Publishers, 1996), pp. 164 and 166.
7. *Poems of Henry Vaughan, Silurist*, p. 59.

314

DE PROFUNDIS (291)

1. *John Bailey 1864–1931 Letters and Diaries*, edited by Sarah
   Bailey (London: John Murray, 1935), p. 294. This is noted by Joe
   Griffiths in 'The Changing World of Walter de la Mare's Poetry',
   The Walter de la Mare Society Magazine, no. 10, January 2007,
   pp. 38–48: p. 47.

Index of Titles and First Lines

(Titles are set in italic, first lines in roman.)